HOW GOD GROWS a PRAYING Girl

A DEVOTIONAL

HOW GOD GROWS a PRAYING Girl

A DEVOTIONAL

JoAnne Simmons
with Jodi Simmons and Lilly Simmons

SHILOH kidz
An Imprint of Barbour Publishing, Inc.

Published by Shiloh Kidz, an imprint of Barbour Publishing, Inc., 1810 Barbour Drive, Uhrichsville, Ohio 44683, www.shilohkidz.com

Our mission is to inspire the world with the life-changing message of the Bible.

Member of the
Evangelical Christian
Publishers Association

Printed in the United States of America.
000181 0220 SP

❃ INTRODUCTION ❃

Hi! I'm JoAnne Simmons, and my daughters are Jodi and Lilly. Our first book together was *How God Grows a Girl of Grace*, and we're writing more encouragement to share, hoping to help you learn more about how to be a praying girl!

We love this simple but oh so powerful verse from the Bible that says just three words: "Never stop praying" (1 Thessalonians 5:17). We hope you realize how incredibly awesome that scripture is! The one true God, who is the almighty Creator of everything, King of all kings, and loving Savior of the world, wants you to constantly pray to Him—about anything and everything! His Word says to never stop! What a great big privilege that is! God is your heavenly Father, and He knows and loves you better than anyone else possibly could. As you read this book, may you learn more about how prayer draws you closer in relationship to Him and how prayer connects you to His love, His care, His strength, and His power for you. May this book help you to learn and grow and be strong as a praying girl, just like we are always learning and growing and getting stronger as praying girls. We sure learned a lot as we wrote this book, and we are thinking of and praying for you as you read it too!

☀ Never, Ever, Ever! ☀

We know it's in the introduction, but we have to talk just a little bit more about how awesome 1 Thessalonians 5:7 is! Think more about it—do you ever get tired of listening to someone talking? Of course you do. We all do. Whether it's because they bring up the same conversation topic again and again or because you simply need some quiet, your ears and brain wear out from listening every once in a while. Sometimes you might not even want to hear from your very favorite people because you just need a break from conversation. And that's okay. You're human! But God is *super*human! He is so far above and beyond what we are capable of, and He does not wear out from listening to us. Never, ever, ever! We are so grateful for that, and we hope you are too.

So no matter what you want to talk to God about, keep it up! He is with you and loves you and loves hearing from you, any time of day or night. You cannot possibly interrupt Him or bother Him in prayer.

*Dear God, I am grateful You never get tired
of hearing from me about anything. Help me
never, ever, ever stop praying to You! Amen.*

❊ WHY? ❊

This is love! It is not that we loved God but that
He loved us. For God sent His Son to pay
for our sins with His own blood.
1 JOHN 4:10

Have you ever heard little kids ask, "Why?" to every single thing a grown-up says? A lot of little kids do, and it's cute—for a while anyway. It can also get old pretty quickly! But it's not bad to continue to ask questions as you keep growing up. You want to have a mind that is curious and eager to learn for as long as you live!

Maybe you've asked *why* you should pray constantly to God. Because He loves you and wants to be close to you forever, that's why! He is the one true God who created all the world and everything in it, including people who are made in His image. He wants all people—that means you too!—to be the best kind of friends with Him. But when the first two people, Adam and Eve, chose to sin and hurt their good relationship with God, that affected all people who would come after them, including you and me. But God made a wonderful plan for people to come back to good relationship with Him. . . .

(Read on to learn more about this wonderful plan, the Gospel. If you already know it, great! We hope you never get tired of hearing about it and sharing it with others too!)

....

Dear God, please remind me all the time
why it's so good to pray to You! Amen.

☀ Life That Lasts Forever ☀

You get what is coming to you when you sin. It is death!
But God's free gift is life that lasts forever.
It is given to us by our Lord Jesus Christ.
ROMANS 6:23

Because Adam and Eve sinned and that affected all people after them and brought hardship and death to the world, God made a way to overcome sin and provide life that lasts forever through relationship with Him. He showed what incredible love He has for people by giving His one and only Son, Jesus Christ, to die to pay the price of sin for every single person. And Jesus did not stay dead! He rose again, proving God's power over death—power that He gives to us when we accept Jesus as the only Savior from our sin and the only Way to God the Father.

The very best prayer anyone can ever pray is a prayer of salvation that goes like this:

Dear God, I know that I make mistakes and bad choices
that hurt myself and hurt others. Those things are sin,
and I am a sinner. I trust that You sent Your Son, Jesus Christ,
as the only Savior from sin. I believe Jesus died on the cross
to pay for my sin and rose again and gives me life that lasts
forever. That's amazing, and I am so grateful! I want to
give my life to You, God, and do my best to live like Jesus.
I love You, and I need Your help in all things. Amen.

☀ Always With You ☀

For we know how dearly God loves us, because he has given us the Holy Spirit to fill our hearts with his love.
ROMANS 5:5 NLT

Though Jesus rose again to life, He did not stay on the earth. He went up to heaven to be with the Father, but He didn't leave us alone. He gave us the Holy Spirit to be with us until He returns to earth again. When we believe in Jesus as Savior, the Holy Spirit lives in us, helping us and guiding us. So as you pray, you can think about how all your thoughts are like a constant conversation with God. He knows each and every thing you think and say and do. No, you will not always act perfectly, but with Jesus as your Savior, you never have to be afraid that God is always watching and listening. That's a good thing! You have the One who *is* perfect with you at all times. Let His nonstop presence with you comfort you and strengthen you as you endlessly talk to Him and ask for His help.

Dear God, help me to remember that You are always with me. You want me to talk to You about everything and ask for Your help too. That is so super cool! Amen.

❧ Really, Everything? ❧

*Learn to pray about everything. Give thanks
to God as you ask Him for what you need.*
PHILIPPIANS 4:6

A lot of really important stuff goes on in our lives, and a lot of little stuff happens too. Does our God of the whole universe really want to hear about *everything*? It seems hard to believe, but He really does! Wow, what a gift that is!

Think about it in terms of love and relationship. Jodi and Lilly and I care about all the things in each other's lives because we love each other so much. You have family and friends you love that way too. And God loves you so much more than even your closest family member or friend, so He cares about every. single. detail. of your life (even the number of hairs on your head, Luke 12:7 tells us!). So anything that is worrying you or anything that is exciting you or anything that is scaring you, remember that He cares and wants to hear about it all—the good and the bad, no matter the size of the problem or the praise.

*Dear God, help me not to think that anything is
too small or unimportant to talk to You about.
Thank You for loving me so much and caring
about everything I care about! Amen.*

Devoted to Prayer

Devote yourselves to prayer with an alert mind and a thankful heart.
Colossians 4:2 NLT

While you should think of prayer as constant conversation with God, it's also important to have specific and focused times of prayer to God. You might already be doing this! Do you pray a blessing at mealtimes and thank God for your food? Do you say bedtime prayers? If you do—awesome! Keep it up! Those are great times to remember to pray!

Our family encourages one another to pray about everything all day long, and we stop and pray together whenever we need to, no matter what time of day. Our focused times of prayer are together before meals, and at night we each take a turn praying out loud before heading to bed.

Whatever your times of prayer are, you can always develop them on your own and with others. Right now, if you're remembering to say thanks to God for the food at each meal, also start telling God other things you're thankful for that happened that day. If at night you're thanking Him for the day and asking for a good night of sleep, also ask Him for help with the things you'll be doing the next day and the problems you're facing and that loved ones are facing. Whatever you're praying to God about and whenever you're praying, keep increasing it. Ask for more faith in Him and for more of His help in your life and for His will to be done. You'll be growing closer and closer to your loving heavenly Father and His love and power for you as you do!

Dear God, please help me to want to keep talking to You even more than I already am. Amen.

✣ WRITE AND REMEMBER ✣

I will remember the things the Lord has done.
Yes, I will remember the powerful works of long
ago. I will think of all Your work, and keep in
mind all the great things You have done.
PSALM 77:11–12

We have a little trouble anytime we go into a bookstore—controlling ourselves! Seriously, there are so many books and items we'd love to buy. Lately there are practically a zillion kinds of cool journals too. We hope you have one of your own. It's great to write down your thoughts and dreams. An even better way to use a beautiful journal is to make it a book of your prayers. Write down your conversations with God and your praises and thanks to Him. Keep lists of the things you are asking of Him. Record when you see exactly how God answered your prayer. When you put dates on each of your prayer journal entries, you have a wonderfully true historical memory book to look back at and see how God is working in your life. And that is a fantastic blessing, not only for you but for anyone you might decide to share it with! If you start this habit while you're young, think of how many awesome journals—full of written records of your love for God and the ways He has shown you His love—you could fill throughout your whole life!

Dear God, I would love to get in the habit of writing
down my prayers to You and recording how You answer
prayers too. Would You help me do this? Amen.

❧ Everyone, Everywhere ❧

It is good when you pray like this. It pleases God Who is the One Who saves. He wants all people to be saved from the punishment of sin. He wants them to come to know the truth. There is one God. There is one Man standing between God and men. That Man is Christ Jesus. He gave His life for all men so they could go free and not be held by the power of sin.
1 Timothy 2:3–6

Like the above scripture from 1 Timothy 2 tells us, it is good to pray for others to know Jesus Christ as Savior. God wants everyone everywhere to know His truth and be saved from sin. Think about all the people in your life, family and friends, who need to ask Jesus to be their Savior. Ask God to help you share His love and truth with them. If you keep a prayer journal, write down their names and remember to pray for them regularly. God loves prayers like these and wants everyone to know Him and not be punished for sin but to have eternal life! What a good heavenly Father and powerful Savior!

Dear God, thank You for wanting to save everyone from the punishment of sin. Please use me to share Your truth and love with anyone who needs to know it, and help me to remember to pray for everyone to be saved like You want! Amen.

❊ STILL AND STEADY ❊

"Be still, and know that I am God!"
PSALM 46:10 NLT

Smartphones are such a cool invention, and we love to use them and play games on them. But they can be really distracting too. Have you ever tried to talk with someone who kept checking their phone for new texts or updates? That's pretty rude, right? A good conversation with a good friend is a focused conversation that shows each other you care and truly want to listen to each other. Prayer to God needs to be the same way—even better, actually!

God knows and understands we have distractions in this life, but we need to work hard to put all distractions out of our minds when we pray and realize exactly who we're talking to in prayer. We should go to God with respect and total devotion because He is the King of all kings who loves us and lets us come to Him at any and all times—amazing!

So when you pray, be still like scripture says. Steady your mind and heart and concentrate on who God is and how much praise He deserves. Tell Him how you love and praise Him. Ask forgiveness for your sins. Thank Him for being your Savior. And then tell Him all your needs and your loved ones' needs. He loves to hear and help with it all.

Dear God, help me to be still when I come to You in prayer.
I want to focus on You and my need for You. Amen.

❊ THE BEST WAY TO PRAY ❊

"Pray like this. . . ."
MATTHEW 6:9

In the Bible, Jesus gave us a specific example of how to pray that you've probably heard of—the Lord's Prayer. In Matthew 6:9-13, Jesus says, "Pray like this: 'Our Father in heaven, Your name is holy. May Your holy nation come. What You want done, may it be done on earth as it is in heaven. Give us the bread we need today. Forgive us our sins as we forgive those who sin against us. Do not let us be tempted, but keep us from sin. Your nation is holy. You have power and shining-greatness forever. Let it be so.' "

This example from Jesus doesn't mean this is the only prayer we should ever pray and just recite it word for word. It means He gave us an example of prayer, and each time we pray we can model it. In all our prayers we should be sincere and know that God is perfectly holy. We should pray for God's kingdom to come and for His will to be done. We should ask for our daily needs to be met and for forgiveness for ourselves and for us to be able to forgive others. We should ask for help not to sin, and we should praise God. Jesus was so good to teach us this way to pray!

....

Dear Jesus, thank You for teaching us how to pray the best way! Help me to model Your prayer every day. Amen.

❊ NO DOUBT ❊

I write this letter to you who believe in the Son of God.
I write so that you will know that you have eternal life now.
We can come to God with no doubts. This means that when
we ask God for things (and those things agree with what
God wants for us), then God cares about what we say.
God listens to us every time we ask him. So we know that
he gives us the things that we ask from him.
1 JOHN 5:13–15 ICB

What an encouraging scripture this is! When we believe in Jesus Christ, we have eternal life and can pray to God with no doubts! And when we ask Him for things that agree with what He wants for us, He cares, He listens, and He gives us what we ask for. So how do we know what He wants for us so that we can pray in agreement? We read His Word and pray to Him and keep drawing closer to Him every day of our lives! As we draw near to Him, He draws near to us. We know Him better and pray to Him better the more time we spend with Him.

Dear God, I want to spend more and more time with You
and continue to learn more about what You want for me.
Help my prayers to match Your will and Your plans! Amen.

❁ BEST BOOK EVER ❁

*Your Word is a lamp to my feet
and a light to my path.*
PSALM 119:105

Do you like to learn about Guinness World Records? We think they're pretty fascinating! And this record is our favorite: "Although it is impossible to obtain exact figures, there is little doubt that the Bible is the world's best-selling and most widely distributed book. A survey by the Bible Society concluded that around 2.5 billion copies were printed between 1815 and 1975, but more recent estimates put the number at more than 5 billion." Wow! There are a lot of great books in the world, but nothing tops God's Word!

The more you learn about the Bible and spend time reading it, the closer you grow to God, the more you grow as a follower of Jesus, and the more you grow as a girl of prayer too! What a win-win-win! You learn more about God and His will, you learn about Jesus' life and how He spoke and prayed, and you learn to pray like the authors of the Bible did—knowing God is the ultimate author because He inspired each of the writers (2 Peter 1:20–21).

So don't ever stop digging into your Bible! It is your light to follow for your entire life.

....

*Dear God, thank You for giving us Your Word, the Bible.
Please guide me with it all of my life. Amen.*

❧ crave ❧

*How can a young man keep his way pure? By living by
Your Word. I have looked for You with all my heart.
Do not let me turn from Your Law. Your Word have I
hid in my heart, that I may not sin against You.*
PSALM 119:9–11

We know the Bible is not like your favorite fiction stories, and it's not a book that always keeps you feeling good or entertained. But it's not your typical book. It's a living and active book from God Himself (Hebrews 4:12), and it's His main way of speaking into your life and guiding and correcting you.

We know sometimes it's hard to keep up good habits of reading God's Word. We have a sin nature that tries to keep us out of good habits and into bad ones. And we have an enemy, Satan, who fights for our attention and wants to keep it on bad and meaningless things instead of on God and the truth He wants us to hear.

So just like you sometimes crave an ice-cold drink of water on a hot day or your favorite food when you're hungry, ask God to help you crave His Word. Ask Him to help you look forward to spending time in it every day, even multiple times a day. Study it and memorize it and keep it in your mind and heart.

....

*Dear God, I want to crave Your Word and a relationship
with You more than anything else. Please help me. Amen.*

❧ sharper than a sword ❧

God's Word is living and powerful. It is sharper than
a sword that cuts both ways. It cuts straight into
where the soul and spirit meet and it divides them.
It cuts into the joints and bones. It tells what the
heart is thinking about and what it wants to do.
HEBREWS 4:12

This scripture about God's Word sounds pretty painful, doesn't it? But that doesn't mean it's bad for you. Think of other things that are painful but good for you, like getting a shot at the doctor's to help heal you or prevent illness. Or getting a good workout in sports or dance, which can be painful to muscles but good and healthy in the long run as you strengthen your body and build skill and endurance.

Like these kinds of things, God's Word can be painful, but it is *always* so good for you. It's painful when it's telling you what you're doing wrong and how you need to change. But if you follow God's commands in the Bible, you will be much healthier in the long run. As you're growing in prayer, ask God to help you not to be afraid of the good pain the Bible causes when it's helping you get rid of sin in your life. Then let God fill up those places with His goodness and love.

Dear God, please let Your Word correct me
and teach me and make me healthy as I
grow closer to You and obey You. Amen.

❋ GREAT RICHES ❋

Those who love Your Law have great peace, and nothing
will cause them to be hurt in their spirit. I hope for Your
saving power, O Lord, and I follow Your Word. I obey
Your Law, for I love it very much.
PSALM 119:165–167

Even though reading the Bible can be painful at times, we know God's Word is always good and always encouraging, like the awesome way it reminds us of God's great and all-powerful love for us: "Nothing can keep us from the love of God. Death cannot! Life cannot! Angels cannot! Leaders cannot! Any other power cannot! Hard things now or in the future cannot! The world above or the world below cannot! Any other living thing cannot keep us away from the love of God which is ours through Christ Jesus our Lord" (Romans 8:38–39).

Over and over, the Bible teaches us of God's great love and His plans for His people. It motivates us to keep living for Him and following His ways. It reminds us that the hard things of this world are not forever—and all who accept Jesus Christ as Savior have the hope of eternal life in a perfect paradise forever. Wow! It's the one and only book we should never want to stay away from. So pray like the psalmist in Psalm 119:162: "I am made happy by Your Word, like one who finds great riches."

Dear God, thank You for Your great love and
encouragement to us shown through Your Word. Amen.

✷ STRAIGHT TO THE THRONE ✷

*We have a great Religious Leader Who has made the
way for man to go to God. He is Jesus, the Son of God,
Who has gone to heaven to be with God. Let us keep our
trust in Jesus Christ. Our Religious Leader understands
how weak we are. Christ was tempted in every way we
are tempted, but He did not sin. Let us go with complete
trust to the throne of God. We will receive His loving-kindness
and have His loving-favor to help us whenever we need it.*
HEBREWS 4:14–16

What intimidates you sometimes—what makes you feel nervous or like you're not good enough? Maybe public speaking or trying out for a sports or dance team or trying to make new friends in a new school. Meeting someone famous might be intimidating too. How cool, then, that because of Jesus Christ, we never have to feel nervous about going to the royal throne of our almighty God, who is the most famous of all! The Bible says we can go with complete trust to God and ask for His help whenever we need it and He will give His love and kindness and favor every time! Knowing that truth, you never need to feel intimidated about anything. God is with you and is helping you, no matter what you face! He wants you to ask for His help with everything. Amazing!

*Dear God, thank You that You allow me to ask
You for help with anything and everything.
Never let me forget that! Amen.*

❧ WHO Can BE against us? ❧

*Since God is for us, who can be against us? God did
not keep His own Son for Himself but gave Him for
us all. Then with His Son, will He not give us all things?*
Romans 8:31–32

If you have accepted Jesus as your Savior and are following Him, God is with you and for you. And like Romans says, if God is for you, who can possibly be against you? You have nothing to be afraid of—no situation or person or test at school or bully or illness or injury can ever be greater than God working in you and helping you. And you only have to call on Him in prayer and believe in His love and ability to help you.

Make it a regular part of your prayer time to praise God and tell Him how great He is. You will remind yourself of what awesome power you have helping you in all things. Pray like this:

*"O Lord, You have great power, shining-greatness
and strength. Yes, everything in heaven and on earth
belongs to You. You are the King, O Lord. And You
are honored as head over all. Both riches and honor
come from You. You rule over all. Power and strength
are in Your hand. The power is in Your hand to make
great and to give strength to all. So now, our God,
we thank You. We praise Your great and honored
name." (1 Chronicles 29:11–13)*

❋ WHEN YOU JUST DON'T KNOW ❋

*The Holy Spirit helps us in our weakness. For example,
we don't know what God wants us to pray for. But
the Holy Spirit prays for us with groanings that cannot
be expressed in words. And the Father who knows all
hearts knows what the Spirit is saying, for the Spirit
pleads for us believers in harmony with God's own will.*
ROMANS 8:26–27 NLT

What's the toughest situation you have been in? What about
the toughest situation a loved one or friend has been in?
Sometimes it's hard to know exactly what to pray for in
those times! We can be thankful that the Bible tells us the
Holy Spirit prays and communicates for us, taking our words
and explaining them to God in exactly the best way. And
God promises to work out everything according to His will
and for our good.

When you're feeling unsure how to pray, tell God
exactly that and keep on praying. Ask the Holy Spirit to
take your words and make them the best they can be before
God, who loves you and will work out what is best for
you and your loved ones every time.

*Dear God, I'm not always sure what to say to You,
but I never want to stop talking to You in prayer.
May Your Holy Spirit take my words and make
them exactly right for You. Amen.*

❈ EVERYTHING FOR GOOD ❈

And we know that God causes everything to work
together for the good of those who love God and
are called according to his purpose for them.
ROMANS 8:28 NLT

The Bible promises that God makes everything work to-gether for the good of those who love Him. But sometimes that doesn't seem to make sense, does it? Like when you hoped and prayed for a particular part in the school play and didn't get it or prayed to make it on a specific team but were told you weren't good enough. Or how about if you've prayed for healing from an illness for a loved one, but that person dies, even though you prayed so hard and will miss them terribly. We know what that's like. It's awful and confusing.

Just because we're disappointed and hurting and can't understand, that doesn't mean God has changed or His promises aren't true. We have to choose to trust Him even more when we don't understand Him. We have to trust that His thoughts and ways are much higher than ours (Isaiah 55:8–9) and that He is working in ways we will not under-stand in this world. But He promises that someday we will understand, and so we keep praying to Him and believing Him and learning from Him.

Dear God, when I'm hurting and confused,
please hold me extra close and show me Your
love in extra ways. I don't want to turn away from
You just because I don't understand You. Amen.

⁂ imperfect and puzzling ⁂

Now we see things imperfectly, like puzzling reflections in a
mirror, but then we will see everything with perfect clarity. All
that I know now is partial and incomplete, but then I will know
everything completely, just as God now knows me completely.
1 CORINTHIANS 13:12 NLT

When you're praying and asking God for answers and not
understanding His ways, 1 Corinthians 13:12 is so important
to remember. Everything in this world is messed up big-time
from the perfect way God intended it—because sin entered
the world when Adam and Eve chose to disobey God. And
the way we see and try to understand is damaged because
of sin too. But God is working out His plans, and at just
the right time He will make all things new and right. Then we
will see things perfectly as He does, and it will be incredible!

Think of what you were like when you were a baby and
toddler. You can't remember much of those days, can you?
And you couldn't understand a lot of grown-up things then
either. As your body and mind are growing and developing, you're learning and remembering and understanding
more and more. That's kind of how we grow as followers of
Jesus. The more we follow Him and grow in Him, the more
we understand—until one day we go to be with Him in
heaven forever and understand everything perfectly.

Dear God, help me to trust You always. Please give
me peace that at just the right time, You will make
everything turn out right and good forever. Amen.

❧ stronger and stronger ❧

"Lord, I have faith. Help my weak faith to be stronger!"
MARK 9:24

When I'm struggling to understand what God is doing or not doing about what I'm praying for, I like to remember a story in the Bible from Mark 9. A father was asking Jesus for help for his son, and it was so hard for the man to imagine that Jesus could do what he was asking. The father said to Jesus, "Have mercy on us and help us, if you can."

Jesus replied, "What do you mean, 'If I can'? . . . Anything is possible if a person believes" (Mark 9:22–23 NLT).

And the father said, "Lord, I have faith. Help my weak faith to be stronger!"

When we pray, we must remember God is able to do exactly what we ask and so much more! He may or may not answer the way we ask or expect, but no matter how God responds to our prayers, our main response to God should be, "Lord, I have faith. Help my weak faith to be stronger!"

....

*Dear God, thank You that I can ask You for more
and more faith. I believe anything is possible
with You. I want to be stronger and stronger
every single day in my belief in You. Amen.*

❧ MUCH, MUCH MORE! ❧

*God is able to do much more than we ask or
think through His power working in us.*
EPHESIANS 3:20

On Christmas or a birthday, have you ever received a whole lot more than what you hoped or asked for in gifts? Or maybe you were working hard to do well on a test at school and when the graded test came back, you realized you did even better than what you expected. Or maybe your parents planned a big vacation and it was way more incredible than what you imagined! Those kinds of surprises are super fun, right?

Every time you pray, think about how God is able to do much, much more than anything you can dream up! You're a kid, so I know your imagination is awesome, and God is even greater and cooler than what you're dreaming! Remember that He doesn't always work in the ways you want or expect, but His plans are *always* better, and He is so trustworthy. He loves you and wants what is best for you in every. single. situation.

*Dear God, when I'm praying I want to use my imagination
and pray to You in big ways. Then I want to remember
that You can do much, much more than anything my
imagination can dream up. I believe You love me
and do what's best for me all the time. Amen.*

❧ WORTHY OF EVERY KIND OF PRAISE ❧

I will praise You, my God and King.
PSALM 145:1

Sometimes you will see God answer prayer exactly like you hoped and prayed for. Can you think of a time like that? What a huge blessing that is! But no matter how God answers your prayers, He always deserves your gratitude and praise, so tell Him. Thank Him with your words. Sing Him your favorite worship songs. Read and repeat beautiful psalms of the Bible to Him, like this one:

> *I will praise You, my God and King. I will honor Your name forever and ever. I will honor You every day, and praise Your name forever and ever. The Lord is great and our praise to Him should be great. He is too great for anyone to understand. Families of this time will praise Your works to the families-to-come. They will tell about Your powerful acts. I will think about the shining-greatness of Your power and about Your great works. (Psalm 145:1–5)*

Get in the habit now of praying and praising through scripture!

....

Dear God, You alone are so worthy of every kind of praise. Thank You for all You have done, all You are doing, and all You will do. Amen.

❊ Thankful For Care ❊

In everything give thanks.
1 THESSALONIANS 5:18

I will never forget a time when Jodi was really little, maybe five years old, and she was sick in the middle of the night. Isn't that the worst—to wake up, feel awful and exhausted, and have to run to the restroom? Ugh! Jodi was throwing up again and again. I woke up too and was with her, getting washcloths and water, cleaning up, and doing what I could to make her feel better. She felt so terribly sick, yet in the midst of her sickness and pain she paused for a moment and said to me, "Mommy, thank you for taking care of me."

My eyes instantly filled with tears as my heart swelled with such great love for my little girl who thought to thank me even though she was sick and hurting. I encouraged her and wanted to bless her so much for showing that kind of gratitude!

I thought later about how much God as our heavenly Father must appreciate and want to bless us when we thank Him for how He helps us even when we are going through a really hard time.

No matter what you might be struggling with, thank the people who are helping you, and more importantly, thank God, who works in and through people to help you. Every bit of love and care you receive ultimately comes from Him!

*Dear God, in all kinds of situations,
thank You for always taking care of me. Amen.*

❊ DON'T STaY AWaY ❊

*Let us not stay away from church meetings.
Some people are doing this all the time. Comfort each
other as you see the day of His return coming near.*
HEBREWS 10:25

We often think of church as just a building we go to, when really the Church is a group of people—all followers of Jesus Christ all around the world! But since we can't all meet in the same place at once, we do have buildings all over the place to meet together.

What is your favorite thing about your church? When I asked Jodi and Lilly this question, Jodi said learning more about God and the Bible, and Lilly said being with friends. Both of those are wonderful reasons to love time at church! We always need to keep learning more about God and His Word, and we need time with other people who love and want to worship God—that's called fellowship with other believers. It's so good to be together, to comfort and encourage each other, to learn together and sing and pray to God together. In fact, the Bible tells us not to stay away from church meetings in Hebrews 10:25!

There are so many types and styles of churches, but the most important thing about any of them is that they must preach the whole Word of God and do what it says—and glorify God by doing so. You glorify God by being part of a church like that! And you also learn and grow in prayer at church. A lot of things in life will tempt you to stop going to church, but don't ever stay away!

....

*Dear God, thank You for Your Church.
Help me to be active in it my whole life! Amen.*

❧ ALL FIVE FINGERS ❧

Pray for all people.
1 TIMOTHY 2:1 NLT

When you were younger and learning to add, did you sometimes use your fingers? And then you started learning you shouldn't use your fingers because you could do it in your head! Lilly learned at church about a cool way to help focus your prayers—and you do get to use your fingers! It's called the five-finger prayer method. Maybe you've heard of it before, and if you google it, you'll find out more about it and different variations of it.

Basically, you use your hand to help guide your prayers to God for others. Your thumb, which is closest to your body, can remind you to pray for the people in your life who are closest to you. Your pointer finger can remind you to pray for people who point and direct others to learning and to help, like teachers, doctors, nurses, police officers, rescue workers, and those who are our elders. Your next finger, the tallest, can remind you to pray for leaders in our nation and our world, like the president and government workers and military personnel and business owners. The ring finger, which is the weakest, can remind you to pray for people who are weak and in trouble and pain and sickness in the world. And finally, your smallest finger can remind you to pray for your own needs.

Dear God, I pray for all people. We all need Your help with everything. Thank You for being Lord and Savior. Amen.

❉ Real Friendship ❉

Come close to God and
He will come close to you.
JAMES 4:8

Have you ever met a new friend at a park or event or activity you're doing and you really liked hanging out with them, but then that time was over and you didn't get to spend time with them again? Even if you thought the new friend was great, you don't really have much of a friendship, do you? Real friendship takes time and effort. Sometimes people call Jesus their Friend because they heard about Him and maybe spent a nice little time with Him at church, but then they don't really work on the relationship with Him. That's so sad, because He is always available through His Holy Spirit and His Word, the Bible. He always wants to grow closer to each of us, and He is the very best Friend ever!

Each one of us must put time and effort into our relationship with Jesus. He is the Savior of everyone who believes in Him, but He doesn't want to be a distant Savior we meet once and never hang out with again. He wants to be the closest kind of Best Friend Forever! We grow closer to Jesus by regularly spending time reading the Bible, going to a Bible-teaching church, serving others in Jesus' name, and praying to Him all the time.

Dear God, I want You as my very best Friend,
and I want to spend time with You every single day.
Thank You for always being there for me! Amen.

❖ serving Jesus by serving others ❖

" 'I was hungry and you gave Me food to eat. I was thirsty and you gave Me water to drink. I was a stranger and you gave Me a room. I had no clothes and you gave Me clothes to wear. I was sick and you cared for Me. I was in prison and you came to see Me.' Then those that are right with God will say, 'Lord, when did we see You hungry and feed You? When did we see You thirsty and give You a drink? When did we see You a stranger and give You a room? When did we see You had no clothes and we gave You clothes? And when did we see You sick or in prison and we came to You?' Then the King will say, 'For sure, I tell you, because you did it to one of the least of My brothers, you have done it to Me.' "
MATTHEW 25:35–40

Reading God's Word in daily devotion time, praying constantly, worshipping God, and learning at church are all ways we grow in our relationship with Jesus. And the above scripture shows us exactly how to be close to Jesus. We serve Him directly when we feed the hungry, give water to the thirsty, share clothes with the needy, and visit those who are sick or imprisoned. Let yourself grow closer to Jesus by serving others in need. Pray for God to show you many opportunities for service all of your life!

Dear God, I want to serve You and draw close to You by serving others. Show me who, where, when, and how. Amen.

❊ Praise God for Creation ❊

*"For in six days the Lord made the heavens,
the earth, the sea and all that is in them.
And He rested on the seventh day."*
EXODUS 20:11

Think of your favorite amusement park and all the fun rides.
Or what's your favorite city to visit? We love to travel and
to go on amusement park rides, and we appreciate all the
cool things about big cities. What God made people capable of designing and building is pretty amazing. None of it
compares with the beauty and awesomeness of His creation,
though! I went to Yellowstone National Park once, just for
a day. (It wasn't nearly long enough, and I can't wait to go
back!) I called it God's amusement park because there were
so many different attractions all in one place, just like at an
amusement park, and yet they were all fascinating natural
wonders that no person could ever come close to creating.
Only God can create supercool natural wonders!

What is your favorite national park or aspect of God's
creation? When you're visiting it or looking at pictures you
took when you were there in the past, spend time in prayer,
thanking God and praising Him for making such beauty for
us to appreciate!

....

*Dear God, You are so awesome to have created such a
beautiful world for us to live and grow in. Draw me closer
to You as I appreciate everything You have made. Amen.*

❊ LOOK INSIDE ❊

*But the Lord said to Samuel, "Do not look at the
way he looks on the outside or how tall he is, because
I have not chosen him. For the Lord does not look at
the things man looks at. A man looks at the outside
of a person, but the Lord looks at the heart."*
1 SAMUEL 16:7

God began by making one man. From him came all the different people who live everywhere in the world.

One of my favorite things about traveling and being in airports is the opportunity to people watch. While waiting for flights, I love to sit and observe all the different people and personalities coming and going in one place. Our amazing Creator God has made people so beautiful and unique, all with different features and shades of skin. But because of sin, people treating other people unequally and unfairly because of appearance or skin color is an ongoing problem.

God loves for us to overcome this kind of sin by reaching out and showing kindness and love to others no matter what anyone looks like! As followers of Jesus, we should be praying constantly for people everywhere to appreciate all shades of skin and all types of appearances and to treat each other equally and respectfully, with kindness and compassion. People tend to look at the outward appearance, but God looks at our hearts (1 Samuel 16:7), and so should we!

....

*Dear God, please help me to look at people like You do,
seeing their hearts and not their outward appearances.
None of that matters. You made and love each individual
person, and You want me to show Your love to them too.
Show me the exact ways You want me to do that. Amen.*

❖ Hearing without Listening ❖

Come and listen, all you who fear God, and I will tell you what he did for me. For I cried out to him for help, praising him as I spoke. If I had not confessed the sin in my heart, the Lord would not have listened. But God did listen! He paid attention to my prayer. Praise God, who did not ignore my prayer or withdraw his unfailing love from me.
PSALM 66:16–20 NLT

Do you ever hear something but not really listen? We all do this, unfortunately. Sometimes if you're sitting in school, you can hear the teacher talking but you're not actually paying attention to what she's saying. Or maybe you heard your parents give you instructions or reminders but you didn't focus and follow through. We've all been there!

God always hears our prayers because He is omniscient and knows and sees all. But sometimes He doesn't seem to pay attention to them. Why is that? Sometimes it's because we are holding on to sins in our lives rather than admitting them to God and asking for His help to get rid of them. Because of Jesus, we can admit all our sins, ask forgiveness, and be free of them—and when we do, God pays attention to our prayers.

....

Dear God, thank You for providing Jesus to free me from my sin. I admit and confess my sin to You. Thank You for taking it away. Thank You for paying attention to my prayers. Amen.

❧ COPYCAT ❧

"When you stand to pray, if you have anything against anyone, forgive him. Then your Father in heaven will forgive your sins also. If you do not forgive them their sins, your Father in heaven will not forgive your sins."
MARK 11:25–26

When we're praying and want God to pay attention, we need God's forgiveness of our sins. And we also need to forgive others for the sins they have done that have hurt us. This is so important. God loves giving grace and forgiveness, and He wants us to do it too. Being a copycat of God and His good ways is wonderful! We should be so grateful for forgiveness of all our own sin that we want to give forgiveness generously to others just like God does.

This can be *sooo* very hard to do. Think of a time when someone was mean toward you and made you mad and hurt your feelings so much! Ugh, it's awful! But with God's power working in you, offering forgiveness is always possible. Even if someone who has hurt you doesn't ever seem sorry and you might never be close friends, you can still ask God to help you let go of the anger and pain they caused and trust that He is working all things out for good.

Dear God, I need Your help to copy forgiveness the way You give it so kindly and so generously. Please help me with this all the time! Amen.

☀ Before You Even Ask ☀

*"Your Father knows what you
need before you ask Him."*
MATTHEW 6:8

If God knows what we need before we even ask Him, like Matthew 6:8 says, then you might wonder, *Why should I even pray at all? God already knows!*

And the answer is because God loves you that much! He wants a close relationship with you that much. He wants to hear from you even though He already knows everything about you and everything you need! Wow, that's the God of the whole universe wanting to be close to you. Amazing! The fact that He already knows everything about you plus everything about *everything* is a reason to want to talk to Him all the more, never a reason to think you don't need to bother praying!

Dear God, You are my good and loving Father. You know everything, and You already know exactly what I need in every situation. I am amazed by Your greatness and that You want to be close to me. Thank You! Amen.

❧ DON'T BE A SHOW-OFF ❧

*"When you pray, do not be as those who pretend to be
someone they are not. They love to stand and pray in the
places of worship or in the streets so people can see them.
For sure, I tell you, they have all the reward they are going
to get. When you pray, go into a room by yourself. After you
have shut the door, pray to your Father Who is in secret.
Then your Father Who sees in secret will reward you."*
MATTHEW 6:5–6

You've probably encountered show-offs in your life, people
who talk mostly about themselves and try to keep all the attention on themselves alone. Jesus talked about these kinds
of people who even use prayer to show off. And He said not
to be like them. Our prayers should be a sincere conversation with our heavenly Father, a time of praising Him and
asking for His help.

Does this scripture passage mean that every single
prayer we pray should be said in secret, when we're alone?
No, but it is making the point that prayer should be sincere
and only to our one true God, and in every prayer we should
want all attention on Him and His power alone, not on
ourselves.

....

*Dear God, help me never to want to put attention on
myself in prayer but to put all attention on You. You are
the only One worthy of receiving prayer and praise. Amen.*

❄ KEEP ON ASKING ❄

Jesus said to them, "If one of you has a friend and goes to him in the night and says, 'Friend, give me three loaves of bread, for a friend of mine is on a trip and has stopped at my house. I have no food to give him.' The man inside the house will say, 'Do not trouble me. The door is shut. My children and I are in bed. I cannot get up and give you bread.' I say to you, he may not get up and give him bread because he is a friend. Yet, if he keeps on asking, he will get up and give him as much as he needs. I say to you, ask, and what you ask for will be given to you. Look, and what you are looking for you will find. Knock, and the door you are knocking on will be opened to you. For everyone who asks, will receive what he asks for. Everyone who looks, will find what he is looking for. Everyone who knocks, will have the door opened to him."
LUKE 11:5–10

Do you wonder if God ever gets tired of you asking for things in prayer? Jesus Himself taught in the Bible that God absolutely does not! What a good Father! Do your parents ever get tired of you asking for things? Of course they do! No human parent could ever say they don't get annoyed sometimes by their children's repeated requests. But God is your all-powerful, never-tiring heavenly Father, and in Luke 11, Jesus tells you to keep on asking!

Dear God, thank You that You never get tired of my requests. I will keep on telling them to You! Amen.

✳ ALWAYS READY ✳

If you do not have wisdom, ask God for it. He is always ready
to give it to you and will never say you are wrong for asking.
You must have faith as you ask Him. You must not doubt.
Anyone who doubts is like a wave which is pushed around
by the sea. Such a man will get nothing from the Lord.
JAMES 1:5–7

Sometimes we have to wait on God to give us what we ask for, but James 1:5 tells us something God is always ready to give us—wisdom! And we sure do need God's wisdom in this mixed-up world, where so much of what is popular in our culture goes against the good truth and guidance in God's Word. So every day—even every minute!—ask God to give you His wisdom. Have faith and don't doubt that He gives it to you. Then use that wisdom in every area of your life! You definitely don't want to be like someone pushed around by the sea. That totally sounds like you'd get seasick, and there could be sharks too—yikes! You want to be someone who is steadily guided by God.

Dear God, thank You for being so generous with wisdom.
I need it every minute, and I'm asking You again now.
I believe You give it and You guide me with it. Amen.

☀ Loving to Learn ☀

*Show me Your ways, O Lord. Teach me Your
paths. Lead me in Your truth and teach me.
For You are the God Who saves me.*
PSALM 25:4–5

You might love school or not so much. With any type of
school, there are probably some things you like about it
and some you don't. Whatever the case, do you think learning ends just after you graduate high school or college? It
shouldn't! Every day of your life, now when you're a kid and
later when you're all grown up, you can wake up asking God,
"Will You please teach me today?" And in every situation,
whether good or bad, you can ask, "God, what do You want
me to learn from this?" And you can repeat those prayers all
throughout your days.

You can let God teach you through your teachers and
subjects and experiences at school and then later on in life
at work or at home caring for your family and in your relationships with others. You can listen and learn from other
people's experiences. You can read good books and find in-
formation from trustworthy sources and seek out wisdom
from others. Most importantly, you can keep learning from
God's Word and sound teaching at church and from other
believers who are strong in their faith and following Jesus.

*Dear God, please help me never, ever stop learning and loving to
learn. You created my beautiful mind and made it capable of so
much. Help me to use it for Your glory. Amen.*

SCHOOLTIME PRAYER

*The fear of the Lord is the
beginning of much learning.*
PROVERBS 1:7

At school you have a lot of opportunities to learn and you have a lot of opportunities to pray too! You might hear talk in the news about prayer being taken out of school, but it can never really be taken out if God's people are there! Any believer can pray silently at any time for God to help in any school situation. You can pray for teachers and staff. You can pray for your classmates. You can pray for opportunities to share God's love. You can pray for God to help you focus and do your best on tests and projects. You can pray for good relationships with classmates and teachers. You can pray for peace and safety at your school. And on and on! No one can ever stop you from silent prayer. Make your school and everything about it a big priority in your prayers, and watch how God works!

*Dear God, I need Your help at school every
day in a zillion ways. Help me never stop
asking for Your love and care. Amen.*

❊ waiT Time = prayer Time ❊

*Wait for the Lord. Be strong. Let your
heart be strong. Yes, wait for the Lord.*
PSALM 27:14

Sometimes you might be waiting on a big change in your
life or help for a big decision, and it seems like nothing is
happening. But God might be doing a lot of work behind the
scenes you have no idea about. So turn your wait times into
extraspecial prayer times. Ask God to show you, little by little, His plans and His purposes. You might be amazed what
He lets you see! And He might answer that He won't show
you exactly what He's doing in your wait times, but you can
pray for more trust in Him even when you can't see what
He's doing.

Do you ever get frustrated that your parents don't always tell you what's going on or keep quiet about something
they say you don't need to know about right now? Often
their silence is for your own good, or maybe even for a wonderful surprise! Even more than your earthly parents, your
heavenly Father is always working for your good, whether
you understand wait times or not. And you can always praise
Him with gratitude for simply being His child.

*Dear God, it's hard to wait and not know exactly how
You might be working behind the scenes. But I trust You
and love You, and I'm so thankful I am Yours. Amen.*

✳ pray for comfort and to be a comforter ✳

*We give thanks to the God and Father of our Lord Jesus Christ.
He is our Father Who shows us loving-kindness and our God
Who gives us comfort. He gives us comfort in all our troubles.
Then we can comfort other people who have the same troubles.
We give the same kind of comfort God gives us.*
2 CORINTHIANS 1:3–4

In our little family, we love to get comfy and watch movies or read together, all snuggled up in soft blankets. Our dogs, Jasper and Daisy, love to snuggle in with us too. It's so comforting and relaxing to just be together. And sometimes we need extra comfort when we're experiencing the really hard and sad things of life.

What is your favorite kind of comfort? Whatever it is, remember that all good comfort comes from God, like 2 Corinthians 1 teaches us. The comfort you need might be through warm blankets and time with family. It might be an encouraging conversation with a friend or your favorite food cooked for you by Grandma when you're sick. It might be some extraspecial alone time with God and His Word speaking directly to your circumstances. And in times when you see others needing comfort, you can remember all that you've received and then be a giver of comfort too!

All the time, you can pray and ask your comforting Father in heaven for whatever comfort you need. And as you see Him answer and provide, ask Him to help you share comfort with others at every opportunity!

*Dear God, I thank You so much for all the comfort
You provide. Help me to share it generously! Amen.*

❋ WATCH AND PRAY ❋

"Watch and pray so that you will not be tempted. Man's spirit is willing, but the body does not have the power to do it."
MATTHEW 26:41

Sometimes we have the very best plans to do a good job with something, and then we just don't follow through. Do you ever plan to keep your room clean without being asked, but then two weeks later you can barely walk across the floor because toys and clothes and projects have piled up? Do you ever plan to study hard and long for an upcoming test but then find yourself quickly cramming the night before? Do you ever plan to have regular quiet time with God and His Word but you keep letting the busyness of the day get in the way?

We are human, and we have struggles and temptations that keep us from doing good. That's why we need to pray for God to help us. We need to tell Him, "I can't do this on my own! Because of sin, I'm tempted to mess up all the time! I need Your great big power working in me to overcome this temptation."

Dear God, I sure do need Your great big power working in me to help with my struggles and temptations. I can't do anything good without You! Please help me with everything! Amen.

❁ Turn Worry into Prayer ❁

"Do not worry."
MATTHEW 6:25

As we're writing this book, we're trying not to worry about some big changes we have coming for our family this fall. And because a couple of years ago we lost a very dear loved one very suddenly, sometimes we worry about losing another loved one or friend unexpectedly. It would be easy to get caught up in these worries, but as each worry pops into our heads, we try our best to turn it into a prayer.

Among many verses in the Bible that tell us not to worry or be afraid, we love to remember Jesus' words in John 14:27: "Peace I leave with you. My peace I give to you. I do not give peace to you as the world gives. Do not let your hearts be troubled or afraid." And Psalm 55:22 says, "Give all your cares to the Lord and He will give you strength. He will never let those who are right with Him be shaken."

We know every person and family have their own challenges and troubles to face, and it's super hard not to worry about them. But you can train your brain to take those worrisome thoughts and give them over to God in prayer.

Dear God, You know my every thought, and You know when those thoughts are worries that are bad for me. Worries steal my peace and trust in You. Please take each worry from my mind and replace it with a powerful and soothing truth about Your strength, Your protection, and Your love for me. Amen.

❋ Always Pray and Never Give Up ❋

*Jesus told them a picture-story to show that
men should always pray and not give up.*
LUKE 18:1

Read and learn from Jesus' example in Luke 18 about always
praying and never giving up:

> *Jesus told them a picture-story to show that men
> should always pray and not give up. He said, "There
> was a man in one of the cities who was head of the
> court. His work was to say if a person was guilty or
> not. This man was not afraid of God. He did not re-
> spect any man. In that city there was a woman whose
> husband had died. She kept coming to him and saying,
> 'Help me! There is someone who is working against
> me.' For awhile he would not help her. Then he began
> to think, 'I am not afraid of God and I do not respect
> any man. But I will see that this woman whose hus-
> band has died gets her rights because I get tired of her
> coming all the time.' " Then the Lord said, "Listen to
> the words of the sinful man who is head of the court.
> Will not God make the things that are right come to
> His chosen people who cry day and night to Him? Will
> He wait a long time to help them? I tell you, He will be
> quick to help them. But when the Son of Man comes,
> will He find faith on the earth?" (Luke 18:1–8)*

*Dear God, this scripture passage shows how much You
want to listen and help me. If people who don't even respect
You choose to help make things right for those who ask them,
how much more do You, my all-powerful, all-loving Father
want to help me? Thank You so much! Amen.*

☀ Let Creation Encourage You ☀

"But ask the wild animals, and they will teach you. Ask the birds of the heavens, and let them tell you. Or speak to the earth, and let it teach you. Let the fish of the sea make it known to you. Who among all these does not know that the hand of the Lord has done this? In His hand is the life of every living thing and the breath of all men."
JOB 12:7–10

Sometimes when I get discouraged about hard things in this world and all the bad things I hear and read in the news, I just need to get outside into God's creation. Looking at a giant tree that grew from a tiny seed, or watching a magnificent sunset spread brilliant colors across the sky, or listening to a bird sing a song that no other creatures sing—these all help put my heart and mind and prayers back in good perspective. I remember that all this beautiful creation came from nothing. God created and designed our world; He created and designed each plant and flower and creature; He created and designed each person in His image; and He created and designed a plan to save us and give us perfect eternal life with Him.

Dear God, thank You for encouraging me through all that You have made. Remind me every day of Your power and Your purposes. Help me to trust that You have the best plans. Amen.

☀ LOTS FROM JUST A LITTLE: PART 1 ☀

Jesus looked up and saw many people coming to Him. He said to Philip, "Where can we buy bread to feed these people?" He said this to see what Philip would say. Jesus knew what He would do. Philip said to Him, "The money we have is not enough to buy bread to give each one a little." One of His followers was Andrew, Simon Peter's brother. He said to Jesus, "There is a boy here who has five loaves of barley bread and two small fish. What is that for so many people?" Jesus said, "Have the people sit down." There was much grass in that place. About five thousand men sat down.
JOHN 6:5–10

When I was a little girl, this account from John 6 was probably my favorite story in all the Bible, and it's still one of my favorites. I like to picture myself there that day. Can you picture it too? How generous of the boy to give up his lunch for Jesus. I wonder exactly what he was thinking when he did. I'll bet he never imagined the miracle Jesus was about to do with his lunch!

Dear Jesus, help me to remember that You can do miracles with anything at all! Amen.

☀ LOTS FROM JUST A LITTLE: PART 2 ☀

Jesus took the loaves and gave thanks. Then He gave the bread to those who were sitting down. The fish were given out the same way. The people had as much as they wanted. When they were filled, Jesus said to His followers, "Gather up the pieces that are left. None will be wasted." The followers gathered the pieces together. Twelve baskets were filled with pieces of barley bread. These were left after all the people had eaten. The people saw the powerful work Jesus had done. They said, "It is true! This is the One Who speaks for God Who is to come into the world."
JOHN 6:11–14

You might be young and feel like you don't have much to offer to Jesus. You might think only when you're a grown-up can Jesus do big things for His glory through you. But that's just not true. As you give your life to Jesus, pray to Him each day like this:

Dear Jesus, I am young and don't have big things to offer You, but I offer what I do have with my whole heart. I trust that You can turn what I have into much bigger things, according to Your will, to show Your love and glory. You are so incredibly amazing! Amen.

❧ Love and Pray for Who? ❧

You have heard people say, "Love your neighbors and hate your enemies." But I tell you to love your enemies and pray for anyone who mistreats you. Then you will be acting like your Father in heaven. He makes the sun rise on both good and bad people. And he sends rain for the ones who do right and for the ones who do wrong. If you love only those people who love you, will God reward you for that? Even tax collectors love their friends. If you greet only your friends, what's so great about that? Don't even unbelievers do that? But you must always act like your Father in heaven.
MATTHEW 5:43–48 CEV

This scripture is a great example of how God's ways are often so opposite of our world's ways. It's popular and easy to love just your friends and family and those who love you and to hate those who hate you. But that's not what God says to do, and it's sure not popular or easy to love and pray for the enemies and meanies in your life. Yet that's what God wants. It seems totally impossible sometimes! But with His help, you can do this, and so can we. It might be a huge struggle at first, but try it out and keep trying! Then watch how God blesses you when you obey His good commands and seek His help to love and pray for enemies.

Dear God, this good command of Yours is super hard to obey, and I sure can't do it on my own. But with Your help, I want to love and pray for my enemies. Amen.

❊ FILLED WITH LOVE ❊

I pray that you will be filled with love. I pray that you will be able to understand how wide and how long and how high and how deep His love is. I pray that you will know the love of Christ. His love goes beyond anything we can understand. I pray that you will be filled with God Himself.
EPHESIANS 3:17–19

So often the troubled and mean people in our lives act terribly toward others because they have so little love in their own lives. So as you're praying for enemies, this prayer in Ephesians 3 is a wonderful one to focus on for them. Of course you can and should pray it for friends and loved ones too. But if you pray it for enemies, who knows how God might completely transform their hearts? They might even end up becoming good friends. What a miracle that would be! God can do anything!

Dear God, please fill my enemies up to overflowing with Your love. Help me to show Your love to them however they need, however You want me to. Amen.

☼ pray together ☼

"For where two or three are gathered together
in My name, there I am with them."
MATTHEW 18:20

Every time I went to pick up Jodi from Sunday school at church last school year, my heart filled up with joy and encouragement when I peeked in the window on the door. I loved seeing the girls in her class standing in a circle, holding hands, eyes closed as they finished their time together. Jodi told me all the girls shared prayer requests and praises with their teachers and with each other and then took turns praying out loud about those needs and celebrations. What a blessing! And then they could remember to pray for their friends whenever they came to mind during the coming week. Knowing that others care about your needs and the things you're celebrating can be super encouraging.

Do you have friends or family members with whom you share requests and pray? I hope so! If not, start today by initiating a regular prayer time with your family. And at church or school or your activities, offer to pray for your friends, and ask them to pray for you too.

. . . .

Dear God, thank You for family and friends and the
times when we gather so we can all talk to You
together! These times encourage me so much,
and I want to make them a habit. Amen.

☀ Turn Away ☀

*Turn away from what is sinful. Do what is good. Look for
peace and follow it. The eyes of the Lord are on those
who do what is right and good. His ears are open to their
cry. The face of the Lord is against those who sin.*
PSALM 34:14–16

The Bible is clear that to have good communication with God
through our prayers, we have to keep ourselves away from
what is sinful. If we've asked Jesus to be our Savior, then we
are right with God because of His grace. But that doesn't
mean we should purposefully choose to lie or cheat or do
anything that goes against God's Word again and again.

Romans 5:20–6:2 (NLT) says, "God's law was given so
that all people could see how sinful they were. But as people sinned more and more, God's wonderful grace became
more abundant. So just as sin ruled over all people and
brought them to death, now God's wonderful grace rules
instead, giving us right standing with God and resulting in
eternal life through Jesus Christ our Lord. Well then, should
we keep on sinning so that God can show us more and more
of his wonderful grace? Of course not!"

*Dear God, I know that because Jesus is my Savior, You take
away my sin. But even though I am saved, I don't want to
purposefully go against Your Word. I love You and want to
please You. Thank You for Your perfect grace. Amen.*

☀ Perfection ☀

*And if someone asks about your hope as a believer, always
be ready to explain it. But do this in a gentle and respectful way.
Keep your conscience clear. Then if people speak
against you, they will be ashamed when they see what
a good life you live because you belong to Christ.*
1 PETER 3:15–16 NLT

If you and your life were absolutely perfect, what would
that look like? Each unique person will have a different
idea of this, and it's kind of fun to think about. It will never
happen on this earth, though, so remember it's just a dream
for now! Only in heaven will you be perfect and have perfect life forever. Only Jesus was a perfect human on this
earth. Because of Him, you never have to worry about
trying to be perfect or pretending to be perfect. If you've
asked Him to be your Savior, then He is your perfection and
you belong to Him.

The hope and perfection Jesus gives is something we
should totally want to share with others, like the Bible tells
us to. Ask God to help you be ready at any time to explain
what it means to believe in and follow Jesus, always in a kind
and respectful way. Ask Him to bring people into your life
who need to hear about Him. And keep living such a good
life in Jesus that no one can speak badly about you, even if
they try!

*Dear God, help me to be ready all the time to share
with others about how perfect You are and why all
my hope is in You to have a perfect forever! Amen.*

❧ pray to be like Jesus ❧

Jesus was healing many people of all kinds of sickness and disease and was putting out demons. Many that were blind were able to see. Jesus said to John's followers, "Go back to John the Baptist and tell him what you have seen and heard. Tell him the blind are made to see. Those who could not walk, are walking. Those with a bad skin disease are healed. Those who could not hear, are hearing. The dead are raised to life and poor people have the Good News preached to them. The person who is not ashamed of Me and does not turn away from Me is happy."
LUKE 7:21–23

Jesus loved and cared for people like no other human ever has or ever will. He healed and provided for the sick and needy. He reached out to the lonely and unwanted. He taught truth and showed people the one and only way to God in heaven.

And if we are true followers of Jesus, then we will do these things too! What are the ways you and your family are doing that now? Or how could you start? Keep asking God how He wants you to care for the needs of others and help spread His truth and hope.

Dear God, please help me to give and to care and to share truth and hope. I want to truly love and reach out to people like Jesus did. Amen.

✢ Special Holiday Prayers ✢

Pray in the Spirit at all times and on every occasion. Stay alert and be persistent in your prayers for all believers everywhere.
EPHESIANS 6:18 NLT

Jodi and Lilly's grandma has oodles of cute decorations for every holiday, and they love to help her decorate her house for each of them. Holidays are all kinds of fun, providing great times for family and friends to get together for parties and gift giving and picnics and egg hunts! They are also special times that can help us remember to pray in special ways. Here are just a few ideas:

> *Christmas*—Give special thanks to God for sending Jesus as a baby to live a human life like us and to be our Savior.
>
> *Easter*—Sing to and praise God that Jesus rose from the dead and offers eternal life! Pray for all people to trust Him as Savior!
>
> *Memorial Day*—Thank God for those who have given their lives in military service to help us live in freedom.
>
> *Fourth of July*—Thank God for our nation and pray for protection and peace.
>
> *Thanksgiving*—Thank God for how He provides and guides. Keep track of your blessings and spend time sharing them with loved ones, thanking God together.

Dear God, help me to remember that extraspecial days like holidays are perfect times for extraspecial prayers to You! Amen.

❊ BIRTHDAY BLESSINGS ❊

Dear friend, I hope all is well with you and that you
are as healthy in body as you are strong in spirit.
3 JOHN 1:2 NLT

On the birthdays of your friends and loved ones, you can pray extraspecial scripture prayers for the birthday girl or boy! Here are some examples:

- "May the LORD bless you and protect you. May the LORD smile on you and be gracious to you. May the LORD show you his favor and give you his peace" (Numbers 6:24–26 NLT).
- "I pray that God, the source of hope, will fill you completely with joy and peace because you trust in him. Then you will overflow with confident hope through the power of the Holy Spirit" (Romans 15:13 NLT).
- "May our Lord Jesus Christ himself and God our Father, who loved us and by his grace gave us eternal comfort and a wonderful hope, comfort you and strengthen you in every good thing you do and say" (2 Thessalonians 2:16–17 NLT).

Of course, you can pray and should pray these for yourself and anyone on any day, but birthdays are especially wonderful days to remember!

Dear God, thank You for creating my family
and friends and for the opportunities to celebrate
their beautiful lives. Please bless them and help
them in all ways, every day. Amen.

❈ WHEN IT'S GOOD TO FEEL YUCKY ❈

*"When the Spirit of truth comes,
he will guide you into all truth."*
JOHN 16:13 NLT

Being carsick is such a yucky feeling! Lilly remembers a time she felt awful in the back of the car, but it didn't have anything to do with motion sickness. The yucky feeling was actually the good kind of yucky that helps us feel sorry for sin and want to make it right. The song "Live Alive" by Rend Collective was playing, and the lyrics about not wanting to "live a lie" reminded Lilly she should confess about a lie she had told. I looked in my rearview mirror and could see the tears on her face, and then she shared with me about the lie, told the truth instead, and said she was sorry to me and to God.

So what a blessing that yucky feeling actually was! We do feel yucky when we are holding on to sin and not confessing it to others and to God and asking for forgiveness. Because He loves us so much, God sometimes purposefully gives us yucky feelings inside through His Holy Spirit. Getting a yucky feeling as a reminder to confess sin is a whole lot better than letting lies and sin get bigger and bigger in our lives! As soon as Lilly confessed and received forgiveness, the yucky feeling was gone! We all should pray all the time for yucky feelings that help us admit our sins and make them right.

....

*Dear God, please help me to choose to live by Your
Word. But when I do mess up, I want to feel yucky
about choosing to sin and holding on to it. Help me
to admit and confess my sins and ask forgiveness
quickly, every time. Thank You for Your grace! Amen.*

❊ Relieved, Forgiven, and Free ❊

If we say that we have not sinned, we are fooling
ourselves, and the truth isn't in our hearts. But if we
confess our sins to God, he can always be trusted
to forgive us and take our sins away.
1 JOHN 1:8–9 CEV

Even after we pray to confess sin and have asked forgiveness
from God and those we've hurt, sometimes it's easy to keep
feeling awful for what we did wrong. But God promises time
and again in His Word that we never need to do that. He
takes our sins far away—as far as the east is from the west,
actually (Psalm 103:11–12)! If God is not holding on to them,
why should we?

Our enemy Satan wants us to focus on our mistakes and
beat ourselves up so that we keep feeling defeated and use-
less. So pray against the enemy and believe in the power of
Jesus to forgive you and take your sin totally away!

Dear God, You promise that when I confess my sins
You take them away and never remember them again.
Help me to hold on tightly to that truth. The enemy
wants me to feel awful and trapped and defeated by
sin, but when I confess my sin, You want me to feel
relieved, forgiven, and free from it! I trust that You
love and forgive perfectly and completely! Amen.

❋ JOINED TO THE VINE ❋

I am the true vine, and my Father is the gardener.
JOHN 15:1 CEV

Jesus used an example of a grapevine to show us how we can produce fruit—in other words, do good things in our lives for God's glory—and to help us understand how God answers our prayers:

> *Stay joined to me, and I will stay joined to you. Just as a branch cannot produce fruit unless it stays joined to the vine, you cannot produce fruit unless you stay joined to me. I am the vine, and you are the branches. If you stay joined to me, and I stay joined to you, then you will produce lots of fruit. But you cannot do anything without me. If you don't stay joined to me, you will be thrown away. You will be like dry branches that are gathered up and burned in a fire.*
> *Stay joined to me and let my teachings become part of you. Then you can pray for whatever you want, and your prayer will be answered. (John 15:4–7 CEV)*

We must stay close to our Savior, following Him daily, reading His Word, obeying His commands so they become a part of us, spending time in prayer, and asking for His guidance in everything we do.

. . . .

Dear God, help me to stay joined to Jesus. That is the very best place to be. Amen.

❧ POWERFUL WORDS: PART 1 ❧

No one can tame the tongue.
JAMES 3:8 NLT

The Bible talks strongly about the power of the tongue:

We all make many mistakes. If there were a person who never said anything wrong, he would be perfect. He would be able to control his whole body, too. We put bits into the mouths of horses to make them obey us. We can control their whole bodies. It is the same with ships. A ship is very big, and it is pushed by strong winds. But a very small rudder controls that big ship. The man who controls the rudder decides where the ship will go. The ship goes where the man wants. It is the same with the tongue. It is a small part of the body, but it brags about doing great things.

A big forest fire can be started with only a little flame. And the tongue is like a fire. It is a whole world of evil among the parts of our bodies. The tongue spreads its evil through the whole body. It starts a fire that influences all of life. The tongue gets this fire from hell. People can tame every kind of wild animal, bird, reptile, and fish, and they have tamed them. But no one can tame the tongue. (James 3:2–8 ICB)

We can do so much good with our words, or we can do so much damage. That's why we need to pray *so much* to have self-control over our tongues!

....

Dear God, no one on earth can control their tongue completely. I need Your mighty power to help me be careful about what I say. Amen.

64

☀ POWERFUL WORDS: PART 2 ☀

If you talk a lot, you are sure to sin.
If you are wise, you will keep quiet.
PROVERBS 10:19 ICB

As we pray for self-control over our words, we can focus on and pray specific scriptures that teach us how to use our words in good, encouraging, wise, and helpful ways. Scriptures like these:

- "Let the teaching of Christ and His words keep on living in you. These make your lives rich and full of wisdom. Keep on teaching and helping each other. Sing the Songs of David and the church songs and the songs of heaven with hearts full of thanks to God. Whatever you say or do, do it in the name of the Lord Jesus" (Colossians 3:16–17).
- "Watch your talk! No bad words should be coming from your mouth. Say what is good. Your words should help others grow as Christians" (Ephesians 4:29).
- "A gentle answer turns away anger, but a sharp word causes anger. The tongue of the wise uses much learning in a good way, but the mouth of fools speaks in a foolish way" (Proverbs 15:1–2).
- "Pleasing words are like honey. They are sweet to the soul and healing to the bones" (Proverbs 16:24).
- "He who watches over his mouth and his tongue keeps his soul from troubles" (Proverbs 21:23).

Dear God, "let the words of my mouth and the
thoughts of my heart be pleasing in Your eyes, O Lord,
my Rock and the One Who saves me" (Psalm 19:14).

❖ WHEN IT FEELS LIKE FOREVER ❖

*Rest in the Lord and
be willing to wait for Him.*
PSALM 37:7

These days it seems like everyone wants everything faster
and faster. We want zero wait time in the drive-through or
checkout line. We want Wi-Fi fast and powerful. We want to
order from Amazon and have our package on our porch in
two days or less. And on and on. Have you ever felt like you
had to wait forever (and sometimes "forever" was actually
only ten minutes!) to get something you wanted or to do
something you wanted to do? We all struggle with this in our
own ways!

In our world, it's hard to work on having patience, which
the Bible says is a fruit of the Holy Spirit working in us. We're
supposed to grow the healthy fruit of patience in our lives,
but how do we do that in such an impatient world? We need
to take deep breaths when we're waiting and try not to get
upset but instead remember that waiting can be good for
us. We need to pray, asking God to give us patience and to
help us trust in His perfect timing!

*Dear God, I tend to be so impatient, and the world
around me doesn't help me much to overcome that.
I need Your help to grow in patience. Remind me what
a good thing patience is and all the good ways You
might be working during wait times! Amen.*

❊ Power to Rescue ❊

So Peter was held in prison. But the
church kept praying to God for him.
ACTS 12:5

It's so important to read the whole Word of God and be reminded of and encouraged by the many examples of God's
work in response to people's prayers. As the church kept on
praying for Peter while he was in prison, God moved to rescue Peter in a miraculous way:

The night before Herod was to bring him out for his
trial, Peter was sleeping between two soldiers. He
was tied with two chains. Soldiers stood by the door
and watched the prison.
  All at once an angel of the Lord was seen
standing beside him. A light shone in the building. The
angel hit Peter on the side and said, "Get up!" Then
the chains fell off his hands. The angel said, "Put on
your belt and shoes!" He did. The angel said to Peter,
"Put on your coat and follow me." Peter followed
him out. He was not sure what was happening as the
angel helped him. He thought it was a dream.
  They passed one soldier, then another one. They
came to the big iron door that leads to the city and
it opened by itself and they went through. As soon as
they had gone up one street, the angel left him.
  As Peter began to see what was happening, he
said to himself, "Now I am sure the Lord has sent His
angel and has taken me out of the hands of Herod."
(Acts 12:6–11)

....

Dear God, I believe You have the power to
do all kinds of mighty miracles! Amen.

❋ Prayer For Your Family ❋

*"Honor your father and your mother, so your life may
be long in the land the Lord your God gives you."*
EXODUS 20:12

It's a big job to be a mom or a dad, so I hope you're praying for your parents. Good parents do so much to take good care of you. You're not always going to get along perfectly with them, but God's Word teaches you to honor and obey them. In what ways do you find it hardest and easiest to obey Mom and Dad? Do you need to work on being willing to obey with a good attitude, even when obedience is hard? You encourage and bless your parents when you obey without complaining, and even more importantly, you please God.

You also help your parents and please God when you get along well with your siblings. So pray for good relationships in your whole family. Think of your family as the best kind of team—all of you with different skills to contribute and everyone valuable and needed. If you're usually fighting and upset with each other, you can't really accomplish anything. But a family working together as a team that loves and serves God is unstoppable!

*Dear God, I need Your help to do my best to always
honor and obey my parents plus regularly pray for them.
I want our family to be a team that works together well
to bring You glory. That's a real win, for sure! Amen.*

❊ More Prayer for Family ❊

But those who won't care for their relatives,
especially those in their own household, have denied
the true faith. Such people are worse than unbelievers.
1 TIMOTHY 5:8 NLT

The Bible is clear that we need to look out for one another in our families, especially the ones in our household like our parents and siblings but also our extended family—grandparents, aunts, uncles, and cousins. As a kid you might wonder what you can do to take care of others in your family, but you can always encourage family members and you can always pray for their needs. At reunions and get-togethers and celebrations, you can make the best of whatever time you spend with your extended family. You can share God's love, and if there is conflict, you can try to help resolve it and be forgiving of others. God placed you in your family. Thank Him for each person and ask Him to help you be a loving member of your family.

....

Dear God, I love my family, and You love them
even more. Please help us to have good relationships.
And please help any family members who don't believe
in You to ask You to be their Savior. Show me what
I can do to share Your truth with them. Amen.

❧ walking in love ❧

Live this free life by loving and helping others.
You obey the whole Law when you do this one thing,
"Love your neighbor as you love yourself."
GALATIANS 5:13–14

Our favorite walks around our neighborhood are at Christmastime, as we look at all the Christmas lights decorating people's houses! It's a chilly time in Ohio (okay, sometimes freezing actually!) but such a fun and beautiful time. We usually take mugs of hot cocoa with us too. Yum!

An even better type of walk around your neighborhood, at any time of the year, is a prayer walk. Focus your mind on praying for the people who live in each house. God wants you to reach out to other people and share His love, and your neighbors who live close by provide a great opportunity for that! On a prayer walk, you can get some healthy exercise plus ask God to show you opportunities to share His love with the specific people He has placed in your community.

Dear God, thank You for my neighborhood and the people
in it. You know and love every single person. Please show
me how You want me to share Your love with them. Amen.

❧ Prayer for Your Church ❧

*Those who believed what Peter said were baptized
and added to the church that day—about 3,000 in all.
All the believers devoted themselves to the apostles'
teaching, and to fellowship, and to sharing in meals
(including the Lord's Supper), and to prayer.*
ACTS 2:41–42 NLT

The Church with a capital C is all believers everywhere, and if you belong to a local church, you have a group of people who are your church family. They all need your prayer too. Every time you walk in the doors of your church, you can pray for the protection of your church and the people who come. You can pray for the pastor and leaders and teachers and employees and volunteers of your church. You can pray for the people who are members and the people who attend. You can pray for your church to preach and follow God's Word and glorify Him in everything. You can pray God brings more and more people to hear His truth and experience His love at your church. You can pray to ask God to show you how you can be an active part of your church.

*Dear God, I pray for my church, my church family,
and all those who need to come to my church to
learn more about You. I pray that You help me to
serve and be active in my church all my life. Amen.*

❄ PROUD PRAISE ❄

*If anyone wants to be proud, he should
be proud of what the Lord has done.*
2 CORINTHIANS 10:17

Our world talks a lot about being proud of yourself, but the Bible teaches we should be proud of God! He is the One who does all good things and gives us the ability to do good things.

Read what Psalm 34:1–8 says and strive to make it true in your own life:

> *I will honor the Lord at all times. His praise will
> always be in my mouth. My soul will be proud to tell
> about the Lord. Let those who suffer hear it and be
> filled with joy. Give great honor to the Lord with me.
> Let us praise His name together. I looked for the Lord,
> and He answered me. And He took away all my fears.
> They looked to Him and their faces shined with joy.
> Their faces will never be ashamed. This poor man
> cried, and the Lord heard him. And He saved him out
> of all his troubles. The angel of the Lord stays close
> around those who fear Him, and He takes them out
> of trouble. O taste and see that the Lord is good.
> How happy is the man who trusts in Him!*

*Dear God, I want to be proud of You alone.
Help me to see how every good thing I
ever do ultimately comes from You! Amen.*

✦ Mary's Praise ✦

The angel said to her, "Mary, do not be afraid. You have found favor with God. See! You are to become a mother and have a Son. You are to give Him the name Jesus."
LUKE 1:30–31

Mary was just an ordinary girl, chosen to serve God in an extraordinary way—by being the mother of the Savior of the world, Jesus! When Mary learned this, at first she was in shock and had some serious questions for the angel sent to tell her the news. But once her questions were answered, she said, "I am willing to be used of the Lord. Let it happen to me as you have said" (Luke 1:38). And when she shared the news with her cousin Elizabeth, she said:

> *"My heart sings with thanks for my Lord. And my spirit is happy in God, the One Who saves from the punishment of sin. The Lord has looked on me, His servant-girl and one who is not important. But from now on all people will honor me. He Who is powerful has done great things for me. His name is holy. The loving-kindness of the Lord is given to the people of all times who honor Him." (Luke 1:46–50)*

We can be like Mary, willing to serve God in any way, even ways that seem impossible at first, and ready to praise Him for His awesome works through His people!

Dear God, help me to be willing, like Mary, to serve You in any way You ask. I praise You and honor You! Amen.

73

☀ WHEN WE NEED TO SLOW DOWN ☀

You must all be quick to listen,
slow to speak, and slow to get angry.
JAMES 1:19 NLT

Sometimes we need a whole lot of prayer to obey what the Bible says about anger. It's just so easy to feel angry and let it quickly overtake us. Anger is not always bad; in fact, sometimes it's quite good. It can help protect us and protect others. Like if a bully were to hit you or someone else, of course you should be mad and try to protect yourself or others so the bully cannot hurt someone again. And Jesus became very angry at times (John 2:13–17), and He is the only perfect human being!

But other times we just get mad and let our emotions take over when what we actually need is to slow down, take a deep breath, and figure out *why* we're feeling so mad. It's not bad to feel anger; it's what we do with it that matters. We need to control it and deal with it in healthy ways and not hurt others with angry words or actions. And if we do hurt others, we need to apologize and ask forgiveness and make things right. Be sure to ask a trusted grown-up for help if you feel like you have lots of anger and don't know what to do with it.

Dear God, sometimes I feel too angry too quickly over
things that shouldn't upset me so much. Will You help me
to slow down in these times? I don't want to hurt others
with angry words or actions. Will You show me a person who
would best be able to talk this out with me? Thank You that
You know all my emotions and You love and care for me! Amen.

❖ unified teamwork ❖

*"May they experience such perfect unity
that the world will know that you sent me and
that you love them as much as you love me."*
JOHN 17:23 NLT

In our family, we're not big into video games, but we do like to play some family fun ones together. Recently we tried one called *Overcooked*. It's a fun, silly game where we need to practice good teamwork to make the right food in time to fulfill the customers' orders.

Good teamwork is necessary in a lot of areas of life. You've probably experienced this in sports or group projects at school. Did you know Jesus specifically prayed for good teamwork among Christians? He prayed for unity, that all of His followers through all of time would be one team with God the Father and Jesus the Son, working together to share God's love and help more and more people believe in Jesus. Here is Jesus' prayer in John 17:20–21, 23 (NLT):

> *"I am praying not only for these disciples but also for all who will ever believe in me through their message. I pray that they will all be one, just as you and I are one—as you are in me, Father, and I am in you. And may they be in us so that the world will believe you sent me. . . . May they experience such perfect unity that the world will know that you sent me and that you love them as much as you love me."*

Dear God, help me to do my part well and promote unity among Jesus' followers so that we can win at sharing Your love and helping others know Jesus as Savior. Amen.

❋ prayer for protectors ❋

*"No one can have greater love
than to give his life for his friends."*
JOHN 15:13

Do you have any family members or friends who serve in the military or on a police force? They are our protectors of safety and freedom, and we should be so grateful for them. You can think of ways to honor and encourage them—things like taking treats to share with your local police station, sending cards and packages to service members who are overseas, and always thanking a person in military uniform for their service. Most importantly, you can pray for their safety as they work to keep others safe and free. Especially pray that each one would know Jesus as their Savior!

....

Dear God, those who work in the armed forces and police forces are so brave and give so much to others, knowing at any time their life could be taken as they work to protect others' lives. Please bless and help and protect them in extraspecial ways. Amen.

FOLLOW THE LEADER

"The Holy Spirit is coming. He will lead you into all truth. He will not speak His Own words. He will speak what He hears. He will tell you of things to come. He will honor Me. He will receive what is Mine and will tell it to you. Everything the Father has is Mine. That is why I said to you, 'He will receive what is Mine and will tell it to you.' "

JOHN 16:13–15

Do you ever wish you had special powers like you see in your favorite superhero movie? Sometimes I think I need a superpower allowing me to see into the future, warning me of danger and bad situations. And then I remember that in a way, all of us who have the Holy Spirit because we believe in Jesus (Romans 8) *do* have that superpower. We can pray like this:

Dear God, I can't see into the future, but I know You can. I need Your Holy Spirit in me to warn me of danger and situations that would be bad for me. Please raise red flags and help me sense Your direction away from what is harmful for me. Point me toward what is good for me, according to Your will. I don't need to be worried or afraid of the future; I simply need to trust and depend on You, Your power, Your perfect plans, and Your love. Amen.

❄ SHOW OTHERS HOW TO LIVE ❄

Let no one show little respect for you because you are young.
Show other Christians how to live by your life. They should be able
to follow you in the way you talk and in what you do. Show them
how to live in faith and in love and in holy living.
1 TIMOTHY 4:12

You might be young, but that never means that what you
do doesn't matter. You can ask God right now to help you
make your life an example to others showing how to follow
Jesus and live in faith and love and goodness. How can you
do that? By respecting and obeying Mom and Dad and helping out at home. By working to get along well with siblings.
By showing kindness and love in everything you do. By being
generous to others and helping take care of the needy. By
doing your best at your schoolwork and in your activities.
By admitting mistakes and asking forgiveness. By loving God
with everything in you and loving others as yourself. By sharing with others that Jesus is your Savior and He wants to be
theirs too. And by following 1 Corinthians 10:31: "Whatever
you do, do everything to honor God."

Dear God, help me to remember that the way I live
my life at every age matters. I want to honor You
in everything and be an example to others of what
it means to truly love and obey You. Amen.

❊ keep growing ❊

And this is my prayer: I pray that
your love will grow more and more.
PHILIPPIANS 1:9

This prayer from Paul for the Philippians continues, "I pray that you will have better understanding and be wise in all things. I pray that you will know what is the very best. I pray that you will be true and without blame until the day Christ comes again. And I pray that you will be filled with the fruits of right living. These come from Jesus Christ, with honor and thanks to God" (Philippians 1:9–11).

We can study and copy this prayer because it applies to all believers of Jesus. And all believers can pray it for each other too. Healthy, true Christians won't ever want to stop growing in love and in understanding of God and His Word.

Dear God, like Paul prayed, I want to have love that grows
more and more; I want to have better understanding and
be wise in all things; I want to know what is best; I want to
be true and blameless; I want to be filled with the fruits
that come from living right. I know all good things
come from You, and I praise You! Amen.

❋ ALL KINDS OF TESTS ❋

Dear friends, your faith is going to be tested as if it were going through fire. Do not be surprised at this.
1 PETER 4:12

Tests at school aren't just the kind with paper and pencil or on the computer. Of course there are those, but you also have tests of your faith at school. There will always be difficult challenges and people to deal with, and you'll be tested in how you handle these situations. Will you pray and let God help in each and every one? Will you do your best and be a good team player when working on group projects? Will you avoid peer pressure to do things you know are wrong? Will you reach out in kindness to the classmate others are picking on? All of these are opportunities to prove your faith and grow your faith.

During these tests, the Bible says you are to "be happy that you are able to share some of the suffering of Christ. When His shining-greatness is shown, you will be filled with much joy. If men speak bad of you because you are a Christian, you will be happy because the Spirit of shining-greatness and of God is in you" (1 Peter 4:13–14).

Dear God, help me to see every kind of test as a chance to prove and show my faith in You. I ask You to help me in all things, and I know You will! Amen.

✴ Like a Lion ✴

*Keep awake! Watch at all times. The devil is working
against you. He is walking around like a hungry lion
with his mouth open. He is looking for someone to eat.
Stand against him and be strong in your faith.*
1 PETER 5:8–9

The Lincoln Park Zoo in Chicago is a very cool zoo to visit.
I was there once in college with a friend, and when we
stopped to see the lion, we got quite the close-up view of
him. He was walking right near the front of his enclosure,
so if not for the glass we easily could have touched him. As
we watched him, he suddenly let out a powerful roar! It was
amazing to hear that sound so close to us, and definitely a
little scary too! I can't imagine meeting up with a lion like
that out in the wild—yikes!

I need to picture that lion and remember that fear as
I remind myself of 1 Peter 5:8–9. We all do. We have an
enemy, the devil, who is like a hungry lion lurking around
with his mouth open, ready to destroy us. The only way to
stand strong against him is to stand strong in our faith.

*Dear God, keep me steadfast in believing in and
obeying You so I can stand strong against the
enemy who wants to destroy me. Amen.*

✷ tears in a Bottle ✷

You keep track of all my sorrows. You have collected all my tears in your bottle. You have recorded each one in your book.
PSALM 56:8 NLT

It's awful that it's true, but our hearts get broken a lot in this world, over lots of different kinds of things. God never intended our world to be full of sadness and sickness and death and pain, but when sin entered the world, so did all those bad things. Through each difficult circumstance that makes us cry, we must always believe how much God cares about each of our sorrows. The Bible promises He is near when we are brokenhearted. He heals us (Psalm 34:18; 147:3); He knows and cares about every single one of our sad tears (Psalm 56:8); and for all who believe in Jesus, He is preparing heaven, where "He will wipe every tear from their eyes, and there will be no more death or sorrow or crying or pain. All these things are gone forever" (Revelation 21:4 NLT).

When you are hurting, pray to God and cry to Him. Let Him collect your tears, and focus on the truth of these scriptures. He will help you keep going and keep finding joy, and one day He will make everything right.

Dear God, please help me when I am heartbroken. I need Your comfort and I need to remember the truth of Your Word. Thank You for caring about every tear I cry. I trust You and want to follow You no matter what. Amen.

☀ Pray for Fruit ☀

But the Holy Spirit produces this kind of fruit in our lives: love, joy, peace, patience, kindness, goodness, faithfulness, gentleness, and self-control. There is no law against these things!
GALATIANS 5:22–23 NLT

If you google search, you can find some really fun songs about the fruits of the Spirit to help you remember them. As you learn and sing those songs, make these fruits part of your regular prayers. Ask God to grow them abundantly in your life and to help you share them with others. And if you write in a prayer journal, keep track of how you see God growing the fruits of the Spirit in your life and whom He has asked you to share them with. You might write something like, *I really needed extra gentleness with my little sister today, and I prayed and God gave it.* Or *I felt like I would have zero self-control over my words when a classmate made me mad today, but I prayed and God helped me choose my words carefully.* If you keep a record, you can look back later and remember and thank God and let your faith be made even stronger!

Dear God, I want to see more love, joy, peace, patience, kindness, goodness, faithfulness, gentleness, and self-control in my life. Please let Your Holy Spirit grow these in my life so I can share them with others. Amen.

❧ NO POTATOES! ❧

*Do you not know that your body is a house of God
where the Holy Spirit lives? God gave you His Holy
Spirit. Now you belong to God. You do not belong to
yourselves. God bought you with a great price.
So honor God with your body. You belong to Him.*
1 Corinthians 6:19–20

What are your favorite ways to get healthy exercise for your body? Jodi and Lilly love to jump on our trampoline (especially when it's raining!), swim, and dance. There are so many fun ways for kids to stay active and healthy. And so many options for healthy foods too!

Sadly, there are a whole lot of ways to grow unhealthy too. Watching too much TV, playing too many video games, and eating too much junk food, to name just a few. These things are fine to enjoy here and there, but too much and they can turn you into a couch potato with major health problems later on.

Start praying now and continue your whole life to see your body the way God sees it—dearly loved and a place where His Holy Spirit lives! He wants you to take good care of this home for the Holy Spirit so that while you're here on earth, you can do the wonderful things He has planned for you to do to share His love.

....

*Dear God, I need Your help to want to stay active
and healthy my whole life. The world has a lot of
ways to tempt me to become a couch potato,
and I don't want that. Amen.*

❈ NO MATTER WHAT ❈

Heal me, O Lord, and I will be healed. Save me
and I will be saved. For You are my praise.
JEREMIAH 17:14

Sometimes no matter how hard you try to stay healthy and take care of your body, sickness or injury comes your way anyway. That totally stinks! Minor colds and such are no big deal, but maybe you've dealt or are dealing with a much scarier illness or injury. If not you, surely you know someone who is, and that person needs extraspecial prayer!

Anyone struggling with illness or injury should learn about the life and faith of Joni Eareckson Tada. Actually, every healthy person should too. She's amazing! I encourage you to read her books and watch her movie and listen to her on the radio or through her website. Her arms and legs were paralyzed in a diving accident at just seventeen years old. Her body that was once young and healthy and able to do so many fun activities was suddenly able to do almost nothing without help. Joni had to work through so much sadness and anger and pain to learn to cope with her lifelong condition of being paralyzed. And she is one of the greatest leaders of faith in our world today, proving again and again for over fifty years in all kinds of physical hardship that she trusts God and sees Him at work in her life through her condition. She has helped countless other people with their injuries and illnesses too. She is so inspiring and someone Jodi, Lilly, and I look up to very, very much!

Dear God, thank You that no matter what illnesses or injuries
come our way in life, You never leave us alone in them. Amen.

❄ NO GRUMPY GIVERS! ❄

Remember this—a farmer who plants only a few seeds will get a small crop. But the one who plants generously will get a generous crop. You must each decide in your heart how much to give. And don't give reluctantly or in response to pressure. "For God loves a person who gives cheerfully." And God will generously provide all you need. Then you will always have everything you need and plenty left over to share with others.
2 CORINTHIANS 9:6–8 NLT

Do you have favorite toys and collections that you can't imagine ever giving up? We all like to love our favorite stuff. But we have to be very careful with this. We should never love any certain things more than we love God and want to obey Him. And that requires a lot of prayer!

Start praying now to love being a giver much more than being a getter. Pray to be a sharer rather than a hoarder. And ask God to help you always be happy to give. His Word says He wants us to be cheerful givers, not grumpy ones who only give because we're forced to because we're afraid we'll get in trouble if we don't.

Dear God, I need Your help all the time to love being a giver much more than I love being a getter. Please grow joy and cheer in me over being generous and sharing with others. I want to remember that every good thing ultimately comes from You! Amen.

❊ Hezekiah's Prayer ❊

"Now, O Lord our God, I beg You to save us."
2 Kings 19:19

Even if you never become a leader of a nation, like Hezekiah was king of Judah, you can be inspired by how he prayed when all the cities of Judah were captured by enemies and everything seemed hopeless.

> *Hezekiah prayed to the Lord, saying, "O Lord the God of Israel, You sit on Your throne above the cherubim. You are the God, and You alone, of all the nations of the earth. You have made heaven and earth. Turn Your ear, O Lord, and hear. Open Your eyes, O Lord, and see. Listen to the words Sennacherib has spoken against the living God. O Lord, it is true that the kings of Assyria have destroyed the nations and their lands. They have thrown their gods into the fire. For they were not gods, but the work of men's hands, made from wood and stone. So they have destroyed them. Now, O Lord our God, I beg You to save us from his power. Then all the nations of the earth may know that You alone are God, O Lord."*
> *(2 Kings 19:15-19)*

God answered Hezekiah's prayer and rescued Judah from the evil Assyrians. (Read on in 2 Kings 19 to find out more.) Let Hezekiah's prayer inspire you to pray like this:

> *Dear God, when everything seems hopeless for me and I feel like I have enemies controlling me, please come to my rescue like You did for Hezekiah. I know You can! Amen.*

❋ WATCH OUT FOR THE WAXY ONES ❋

When we obey God, we are sure that we know him. But if we claim to know him and don't obey him, we are lying and the truth isn't in our hearts. We truly love God only when we obey him as we should, and then we know that we belong to him. If we say we are his, we must follow the example of Christ.
1 JOHN 2:3–6 CEV

If you've ever gone to a wax museum, you've seen how much something that is fake can look like the real deal. It's amazing how lifelike those wax statues can be! The Bible talks about hypocritical people who say they know Jesus, but actually they are not real-deal followers of Him. As you get to know and observe them, you find they don't want to obey the Bible and live like Jesus did. We need to pray and be on the lookout for these people and not let them influence us or our faith. And it's so important to keep reading and studying God's Word so we can constantly compare what we are learning with how people are living—especially how we ourselves are living. If we say we know and love Jesus, we should want to be known as real-deal followers of Him, never waxy fake ones!

Dear God, help me to obey You and live like Jesus did. I want to be known for truly loving and living for You. Amen.

☀ pray in line ☀

We thank God for you all the
time and pray for you.
1 THESSALONIANS 1:2

Do you spend a lot of time waiting in line? At school and in the cafeteria and at the bus stop? In the checkout aisle at the store with Mom and Dad? Or while you're running errands with them to the bank or post office? I'm not sure I'd ever want to count up all the minutes in my life I've spent waiting in line—I've done a whole lot of it by now. At first it seems like such a waste of time—until you choose to be productive during these moments.

One thing you can always do in lines is use the time to pray! That's never, ever a waste of time! Pray for your own needs and the needs of others, and you can totally pray for the strangers in line with you too; in your mind you can ask God to bless them and help them with whatever their needs and challenges are. Once while I was in line for doughnuts (that's a fun line, for sure!) I felt a strong sense of needing to pray for everyone who was in the doughnut shop with me. I don't know why exactly or how God answered those prayers, but I'm thankful for the chance to be productive in prayer anytime, anywhere!

....

Dear God, please remind me that line time
doesn't ever have to be wasted time. You are
with me and I can always talk with You about
my needs and the needs of others too. Amen.

❧ DON'T JUST DOODLE AND DAYDREAM ❧

Obey the Word of God. If you hear only and do not act,
you are only fooling yourself. Anyone who hears the Word
of God and does not obey is like a man looking at his face
in a mirror. After he sees himself and goes away, he forgets
what he looks like. But the one who keeps looking into God's
perfect Law and does not forget it will do what it says and
be happy as he does it. God's Word makes men free.
JAMES 1:22–25

You could go to school every single day for the rest of your life and never learn anything new—if you choose not to focus. You could just doodle on your paper and daydream and be bored and not care one bit about learning the good things you need to know. I think that sounds like a terrible idea and a total waste of time. I hope it does to you too!

The same is true every time you read God's Word and go to church. You can choose not to focus and care, but then you're totally wasting your time. How sad, right?

Instead, every time you have the chance, you can pray and ask God to help you focus on His Word, learn from His Word, obey His Word, and be a doer of His Word. Then God will help you live your very best life.

....

Dear God, help me pay attention every time I have the chance
to learn more about You, when I read Your Word and when
I'm learning at church and with my family. I want to be
Your true follower and a doer of Your Word! Amen.

❋ DON'T BE LIKE A WEED ❋

*And now, just as you accepted Christ Jesus as your Lord,
you must continue to follow him. Let your roots grow
down into him, and let your lives be built on him. Then
your faith will grow strong in the truth you were taught,
and you will overflow with thankfulness.*
COLOSSIANS 2:6–7 NLT

I'm not really a fan of pulling weeds, especially weeds with prickly stems—ouch! Definitely need the gardening gloves for those! One thing I'm always thankful for when pulling weeds is that their roots are shallow and they're usually easy to pull away from the soil they're growing in.

A favorite scripture of mine that I love to pray for Jodi and Lilly (and myself and others too—including you right now too as I write this!) is the scripture about roots in Colossians 2:6–7. Asking Jesus to be our Savior is the first wonderful step in a wonderful life of following Him and letting our roots grow into Him and His truth, so strong that nothing can pull us away from Jesus. We don't ever want to be like weeds that can easily be pulled out of our life of following our Savior.

*Dear God, I sure don't want to be like a weed that
can easily be pulled away from real life in You.
Help me to be like the sturdiest, tallest tree with
my roots grown strong and deep into You. Amen.*

❧ MORE ABOUT ROOTS ❧

"A farmer went out to plant his seed. As he scattered it across his field, some seed fell on a footpath, where it was stepped on, and the birds ate it. Other seed fell among rocks. It began to grow, but the plant soon wilted and died for lack of moisture. Other seed fell among thorns that grew up with it and choked out the tender plants. Still other seed fell on fertile soil. This seed grew and produced a crop that was a hundred times as much as had been planted!"
LUKE 8:5–8 NLT

Jesus told this parable or teaching story to help us learn even more about having good strong roots. And then He explained the parable this way:

"The seed is God's word. The seeds that fell on the footpath represent those who hear the message, only to have the devil come and take it away from their hearts and prevent them from believing and being saved. The seeds on the rocky soil represent those who hear the message and receive it with joy. But since they don't have deep roots, they believe for a while, then they fall away when they face temptation. The seeds that fell among the thorns represent those who hear the message, but all too quickly the message is crowded out by the cares and riches and pleasures of this life. And so they never grow into maturity. And the seeds that fell on the good soil represent honest, good-hearted people who hear God's word, cling to it, and patiently produce a huge harvest." (Luke 8:11–15 NLT)

....

*Dear God, help me to be that last kind of seed—
one of the people with deep roots in You! Amen.*

❊ OUT OF TROUBLE ❊

*I cried to the Lord in my trouble, and He
answered me and put me in a good place.*
PSALM 118:5

Once when we were at the beach, Lilly and Jodi dug a
deep hole and then Lilly decided to try to crawl headfirst
into it. Soon she got stuck with her legs kicking in the
air, and Jodi and I laughed hysterically (which Lilly didn't
appreciate!) before we helped pull her out. She wasn't
in any real danger, but she did feel like she was headfirst in
quite a troublesome situation.

Unfortunately, we may experience much worse problems than just being stuck in a sandy hole. You've probably
experienced some. How did God help you out of them?
Psalm 118 encourages us that we can always cry out to God
in our troubles and He will help us out of them and into a
good place. It goes on to say, "The Lord is with me. I will not
be afraid of what man can do to me. The Lord is with me. He
is my Helper. I will watch those lose who fight against me. It
is better to trust in the Lord than to trust in man. It is better
to trust in the Lord than to trust in rulers" (Psalm 118:6–9).

. . . .

*Dear Lord, I trust You more than any person or leader.
I know You are always with me, and I don't need to be afraid of
anyone. When I'm in trouble, please help me to get out of it and
get into a good place. Thank You! Amen.*

❧ PUBLIC Prayer ❧

Remember to pray for all Christians. Pray for me also.
Pray that I might open my mouth without fear.
EPHESIANS 6:18–19

Just recently on vacation in St. Augustine, Florida, Jodi, Lilly, their dad, and I were praying together right before we ate our yummy seafood. And then a lady at the table next to us came over to thank us for praying. She said it was so encouraging to see us do that in public. We were so blessed and encouraged to be a blessing and encouragement to her!

As Christians in the USA where we are totally free to worship and pray to God in public, we should be doing this all the more. There are Christians all around the world who live in places where it's very dangerous to be a follower of Jesus and read the Bible. Unless we've been there, it's hard to even imagine how awful that must be. They desperately need our prayers, all the time. And all the more, then, because they cannot pray in public, we should be grateful we never have to hide our faith and our prayers. And we should share our faith and our prayers, even if simply by bowing our heads and praying aloud, sincerely and humbly, before a meal in a public place to our one true God and our Savior, Jesus Christ.

Dear God, help me never to be scared to pray to You out loud and read my Bible in any public place, especially in a nation where I am totally free to do so! I pray for Your extraspecial closeness and care for those Christians all around the world who are in great danger because they follow You. Protect them and strengthen them, please! Amen.

❊ keep Learning from Daniel ❊

*He got down on his knees three times each day, praying
and giving thanks to his God, as he had done before.*
DANIEL 6:10

Daniel in the lions' den is a pretty popular story, and even
if we think we know it well, it's good to go back and learn
from Daniel again and again. Even though Daniel's enemies,
who were extremely jealous of him, convinced the king to
write a law that said it was illegal for Daniel to pray to anyone other than the king of their time, King Darius, Daniel
continued to pray to the one true God. And as punishment
for breaking the law, he was thrown into a den of hungry
lions. But because Daniel never stopped praying, he was able
to witness an amazing miracle—God shut the mouths of the
lions so they didn't harm Daniel! And even more, the next
day King Darius was so astonished by this miracle that he
chose to believe in God and announced that all the people
of his nation should too! "He wrote, 'May you have much
peace! I make a law that all those under my rule are to fear
and shake before the God of Daniel. For He is the living
God and He lives forever. His nation will never be destroyed
and His rule will last forever. He saves and brings men out of
danger, and shows His great power in heaven and on earth.
And He has saved Daniel from the power of the lions'"
(Daniel 6:25–27).

> *Dear God, help me to have great courage like Daniel,
> who never stopped praying to You, even when he was
> in great danger. Please also let me see great miracles
> happen when I follow You no matter what! Amen.*

❀ Three Super Brave Guys ❀

*"There are certain Jews whom you have chosen as leaders
over the land of Babylon. Their names are Shadrach,
Meshach, and Abed-nego. These men have not listened
to you, O king. They do not serve your gods or worship
the object of gold which you have set up."*
DANIEL 3:12

Another famous story we need to revisit often is one of
Daniel's friends with such interesting names—Shadrach,
Meshach, and Abed-nego. Even though they were about to
be thrown into a fire so hot no one could even get near it
without dying, they totally refused to give up their faith in
the one true God to worship a false god. God gave them
such courage that they were able to say to King Nebuchadnezzar, "If we are thrown into the fire, our God Whom we
serve is able to save us from it. And He will save us from
your hand, O king. But even if He does not, we want you to
know, O king, that we will not serve your gods or worship the
object of gold that you have set up" (Daniel 3:17–18).

"*Even if He does not,*" they said. Don't miss that. It's not
that they didn't believe God had the power to save them.
But they trusted that God's will is always best, no matter
what He decides.

....

*Dear God—wow!—Shadrach, Meshach,
and Abed-nego were so very brave. Please help
me to have trust like they did that even if You
choose not to answer my prayer, I will never stop
believing in You! You are always good and right! Amen.*

96

☀ More About Three Super Brave Guys ☀

The three men were still tied up when they fell into the fire.
DANIEL 3:23

Shadrach, Meshach, and Abed-nego were thrown into the fire. But was that the end for them? No way! God was about to do something no one could have imagined.

Then King Nebuchadnezzar was very surprised and stood up in a hurry. He said to his leaders, "Did we not throw three men who were tied up into the fire?" They answered, "That is true, O king." He said, "Look! I see four men loose and walking about in the fire without being hurt! And the fourth one looks like a son of the gods (or the Son of God)!" Then Nebuchadnezzar came near the door where the fire was burning, and said, "Shadrach, Meshach and Abed-nego, servants of the Most High God, come out! Come here!" . . . The captains, leaders, rulers, and the king's important men gathered around and saw that the fire had not hurt the bodies of these three men. Their hair was not burned. Their clothes were not burned. They did not even smell like fire. Nebuchadnezzar said, "Praise be to the God of Shadrach, Meshach, and Abed-nego. He has sent His angel and saved His servants who put their trust in Him. . . . For there is no other god who is able to save in this way." (Daniel 3:24–29)

Dear God, You are amazing! No one is able to save like You! While You didn't stop Shadrach, Meshach and Abed-nego from being thrown into the fire, You also never left them and never stopped protecting them. I trust You will always be with me and helping me too, in any hard thing I have to go through. When I stay strong in my faith in You, please let others see Your miracles and worship You too! Amen.

✸ prayer for those who are wearing out ✸

This is the reason we do not give up. Our human body is wearing out. But our spirits are getting stronger every day. The little troubles we suffer now for a short time are making us ready for the great things God is going to give us forever.
2 CORINTHIANS 4:16–17

Who are the elderly people in your life? Maybe great-grandparents or great-aunts and great-uncles? Maybe you have family members or friends you visit in a nursing home, or an elderly neighbor. If you spend any time around elderly people, you can't help but see the truth of 2 Corinthians 4:16—human bodies definitely wear out.

So pray and ask God how you can be an extraspecial blessing to the elderly people in your life. Visit them, help them, chat with them, make cards for them, and encourage them in whatever ways you can. Most importantly, remind them that if they know Jesus as Savior, their spirits are getting stronger every day, and the troubles for human bodies on this earth are just for a short time. God is going to give great things in heaven forever!

Dear God, please help me to be a big help and encouragement to the elderly people in my life. Show me what I can do for them and how best to share Your truth and love with them. Amen.

❧ WINDS AND WAVES ❧

*Jesus got into a boat. His followers followed Him.
At once a bad storm came over the lake. The waves
were covering the boat. Jesus was sleeping. His followers
went to Him and called, "Help us, Lord, or we will die!"*
MATTHEW 8:23–25

We had some crazy thunderstorms at our house one night while I was working on this book. Shake-the-house crazy! The lightning flashes were so bright and the thunder so loud and powerful, it was pretty scary! In any storms that scare you, remember that Jesus has total power to protect. He can stop a storm with just His words if He chooses to, so of course He can keep you safe.

"He said to them, 'Why are you afraid? You have so little faith!' Then He stood up. He spoke sharp words to the wind and the waves. Then the wind stopped blowing. Then men were surprised and wondered about it. They said, 'What kind of a man is He? Even the winds and the waves obey Him' " (Matthew 8:26–27).

*Dear Jesus, You are so powerful to be able to just
speak and stop the winds and the waves immediately.
I don't ever want to stop being amazed by You! Help
me to have great faith and never be afraid! Amen.*

☀ Solomon's Prayer: Part 1 ☀

The Lord came to Solomon in a special dream in Gibeon during the night. God said, "Ask what you wish Me to give you."
1 Kings 3:5

Solomon loved God, and God gave him an extraordinary opportunity. God came to Solomon in a special dream and told Solomon he could ask Him for anything he wished! Wow!
Here's what Solomon said:

"You have shown great loving-kindness to Your servant David my father because he was faithful and right and good and pure in heart before You. And You have kept for him this great and lasting love. You have given him a son to sit on his throne this day. Now, O Lord my God, You have made Your servant king in place of my father David. But I am only a little child. I do not know how to start or finish. Your servant is among Your people which You have chosen. They are many people. There are too many people to number. So give Your servant an understanding heart to judge Your people and know the difference between good and bad. For who is able to judge Your many people?" (1 Kings 3:6–9)

Solomon could have asked God for any selfish thing, but he asked to have understanding and to be able to judge right from wrong wisely.

Dear God, help me to be like Solomon and ask You for understanding and wisdom. I want to keep on asking for more and more every day. Amen.

☀ SOLOMON'S Prayer: Part 2 ☀

It pleased the Lord that Solomon had asked this.
1 KINGS 3:10

God was very happy with Solomon for his request for understanding:

> God said to him, "You have asked this, and have not asked for a long life for yourself. You have not asked for riches, or for the life of those who hate you. But you have asked for understanding to know what is right. Because you have asked this, I have done what you said. See, I have given you a wise and understanding heart. No one has been like you before, and there will be no one like you in the future. I give you what you have not asked, also. I give you both riches and honor. So there will be no king like you all your days. And if you walk in My ways and keep My Laws and Word as your father David did, I will allow you to live a long time." (1 Kings 3:11–14)

We can learn so much from Solomon's prayer. When he prayed to know and do what was right according to God's ways, God not only happily gave him great wisdom but also blessed him with great riches and honor!

*Dear God, thank You for the example of Solomon
and the way You blessed him so much beyond what
he expected when he chose to pray for understanding
and right judgment instead of selfish things. Amen.*

❊ proactive prayer ❊

Look to the Lord and ask for His strength.
Look to Him all the time.
1 CHRONICLES 16:11

When we were brainstorming ideas for this book, we went to a little café and tried mochi ice cream for the first time. Mochi ice cream is ice cream that's wrapped in Japanese sticky rice dough.

Lilly took one bite and made a hilarious disgusted face. She didn't like it—not one bit! Her reaction and the funny look on her face made Jodi and me laugh until our sides hurt!

According to wordcentral.com, to react to something means "to act or behave in response."

On the other hand, to be proactive means "to act in anticipation of future problems, needs, or changes."

Lilly's big reaction to the mochi ice cream made us think about how some people pray only as a reaction to life's negative events. Like only praying to God when you're already sick rather than also praying ahead of time to stay healthy. Or only praying to God in emergency situations or natural disasters rather than praying to God all the time in relationship with Him.

Of course we should pray in reaction to life's events. We need God's help! But we should also be strongly *proactive* in our prayers, building a close relationship with God while talking with Him all the time about everything—past, present, and future, not just when we find ourselves in desperate need of help.

....

Dear God, help me to be a proactively praying girl
who loves to talk to You in all kinds of situations. Amen.

❖ MISSIONARIES EVERYWHERE ❖

"But you will receive power when the Holy Spirit comes into your life. You will tell about Me in the city of Jerusalem and over all the countries of Judea and Samaria and to the ends of the earth."
ACTS 1:8

Missionaries aren't just people who travel the world and live in foreign countries to tell people about Jesus. We are all missionaries everywhere we go and with our friends who are not believers. The Great Commission is for all of us to do as Jesus said: "Go and make followers of all the nations. Baptize them in the name of the Father and of the Son and of the Holy Spirit. Teach them to do all the things I have told you" (Matthew 28:19–20).

Every believer should always be looking for and asking God for opportunities to share our faith and be ready to explain it. But some people (maybe you someday!) do feel called specifically to leave their original countries and go make a new country their permanent home in order to share the Gospel of Jesus with the people there. Being a foreign missionary takes a lot of courage, and these individuals need a lot of support.

If you don't already know, find out which missionaries your church supports and commit to praying especially for them. You also might want to write them letters to encourage them and get to know them!

Dear God, thank You for people who are willing to travel far away and make their homes in all-new places to share the Gospel and help build Your kingdom. Remind me to pray for them regularly! Amen.

❊ Healthy Prayers ❊

Give all your worries to Him
because He cares for you.
1 PETER 5:7

Jodi and Lilly go to a dentist who only cares for kids, where there are a lot of things to be thankful for—super nice staff, movies to watch on the ceiling while their teeth are examined and cared for, and prizes to choose at the end of the visit. Sometimes I wish there were dentists for grown-ups who did these fun things too!

No matter what type of doctor visit you may have, you can take time to pray while you are there, giving thanks for the opportunity to receive good medical care. So many people in the world can't afford good care or don't have any dentists or doctors nearby, so simply being able to go to a doctor to help keep you healthy means you are very blessed!

Dear God, even if I don't like doctor or dentist
visits very much, help me to be thankful for the
care I have access to. And You know my body and
my health best of all, so please guide medical
professionals as they help take care of me. Amen.

❧ More Healthy Prayers ❧

Don't look out only for your own interests,
but take an interest in others, too.
PHILIPPIANS 2:4 NLT

As you're waiting in a doctor's office, it's not okay to ask others what they are there for. That would be too nosy, for sure! But during your wait time, you can look around discreetly and in your mind pray for the people around you. Whether they are there just to get a checkup or to be treated for an illness, they have worries and problems like every person does. Pray that the medical staff will be able to help them and make them feel better quickly. Most importantly, pray that they know the very best Healer of all—Jesus—as their Savior. Who knows how God might answer those prayers!

Jodi, Lilly, and I also like to say a quick prayer anytime we hear a siren from an emergency vehicle like an ambulance or fire truck. In our minds or out loud, we pray, "God, we don't know what that situation is, but You do. Please help the people who are hurt or in danger, and please guide the people who are on their way to help."

Dear God, You know our bodies and our needs better
than anyone, and we thank You for how You have gifted
medical professionals and rescue workers to be helpers.
Please work through them to heal people from sickness
and protect people from danger. Amen.

❋ Like Talking to a Friend ❋

*Inside the Tent of Meeting, the Lord would speak
to Moses face to face, as one speaks to a friend.*
Exodus 33:11 NLT

There is so much to learn from Moses' life as recorded in
the Bible. He had great favor with God, meaning God paid
special attention to Moses and delighted in him. Scripture
tells us God would speak to Moses face-to-face like one
speaks to a friend! Yet later in Exodus 33, we learn that Moses could not look directly at God's face because His glory
is just too great! Reading this passage reminds us how awesome our God is and how He wants to be in close relationship with His people.

We can humbly ask to have great favor with God while
we respect and follow His Word. Pray like Moses: "If it is true
that you look favorably on me, let me know your ways so I
may understand you more fully and continue to enjoy your
favor" (Exodus 33:13 NLT).

*Dear God, I want to make You happy and have Your
favor on me. I humbly ask You to delight in me as I
obey You. Please help me to grow in Your ways and
understand You more every day. Amen.*

❋ UNGRIP THOSE FISTS! ❋

"Give, and it will be given to you.
You will have more than enough."
LUKE 6:38

I love the example I've heard many times that you can't accept new gifts from God if you keep a tight fist around what you already have. An open hand that shares is one that can receive new gifts. As you receive every kind of gift in life, whether money or a birthday gift or the gift of a special talent, ask God to help you be generous with it and use it in a way that brings praise and glory to Him!

Read and remember these scriptures inspiring us to give and give and give some more!

- "I showed you in all things that you should work as I did and help the weak. I taught you to remember the words of Jesus. He said, 'It is more blessed to give than to receive' " (Acts 20:35 ICB).
- "Don't forget to do good and to share with those in need. These are the sacrifices that please God" (Hebrews 13:16 NLT).
- "Give freely and become more wealthy; be stingy and lose everything. The generous will prosper; those who refresh others will themselves be refreshed" (Proverbs 11:24–25 NLT).

Dear God, please ungrip my fists from the gifts
You give me. Help me to love giving and sharing
and watching how You give in return. Amen.

❄ Keep On Going ❄

*We can rejoice, too, when we run into problems and trials,
for we know that they help us develop endurance. And endurance
develops strength of character, and character strengthens our
confident hope of salvation. And this hope will not lead to
disappointment. For we know how dearly God loves us, because
he has given us the Holy Spirit to fill our hearts with his love.*
ROMANS 5:3–5 NLT

Jodi was sick on vacation recently, and it was such a bummer when there was so much fun stuff to do. She was feeling yucky with a fever, but we prayed and God helped her keep on going through the tour we had planned that day. Then later she got to rest and began to feel better.

Even little tests of our endurance let us experience how God gives us strength we don't have on our own. And that builds our faith that He will always provide and help us through tougher times in the future. The next opportunity to build endurance might be a bigger problem or trial. But if we pray and depend on God through every kind of trouble, He will be building our character and hope in Him— hope that will never disappoint us!

*Dear God, help me to rejoice in problems and suffering.
It's so hard sometimes, but You want me to learn to depend
on You through them, and that kind of dependence is such
a blessing! Thank You for loving me so well. Amen.*

☀ WITH JUST a WORD ☀

"Only speak the word, and my servant will be healed."
MATTHEW 8:8

When we pray, we need to remember the example of the army captain in the book of Matthew in the Bible. He had such great faith that Jesus only had to say the word and his servant would be healed:

> *Jesus came to the city of Capernaum. A captain of the army came to Him. He asked for help, saying, "Lord, my servant is sick in bed. He is not able to move his body. He is in much pain." Jesus said to the captain, "I will come and heal him." The captain said, "Lord, I am not good enough for You to come to my house. Only speak the word, and my servant will be healed. I am a man who works for someone else and I have men working under me. I say to this man, 'Go!' and he goes. I say to another, 'Come!' and he comes. I say to my servant, 'Do this!' and he does it."*
>
> *When Jesus heard this, He was surprised and wondered about it. He said to those who followed Him, "For sure, I tell you, I have not found so much faith in the Jewish nation. . . ." Jesus said to the captain, "Go your way. It is done for you even as you had faith to believe." The servant was healed at that time. (Matthew 8:5–10, 13)*

....

Dear God, please grow my faith in You to be as strong as that of the captain in Matthew 8. I know You can just say the word and make a miracle happen! Amen.

❧ Brand-New Brain ❧

*Take hold of every thought
and make it obey Christ.*
2 Corinthians 10:5

Have you ever been studying for a big history test and filling your brain with all the little details you need to remember until you're pretty sure it's about to explode with facts and dates and names? You might feel like you need a big mental break after the test is done, right? A total mind renewal or a brand-new brain!

Because we live in a world full of unbelievers, sometimes we spend too much time studying what they do and say and think, and soon that seems to be all that's filling our brains and we even start to copy them. In those moments, we need a brain renewal, and God is the One to give it! His Word says, "Do not act like the sinful people of the world. Let God change your life. First of all, let Him give you a new mind. Then you will know what God wants you to do. And the things you do will be good and pleasing and perfect" (Romans 12:2).

Dear God, when my brain is filling up with the things of this world too much, please refresh me with a new mind that is focused on You and what You want for my life! Amen.

❊ praying the names of god ❊

His name will be called Wonderful, Teacher, Powerful God,
Father Who Lives Forever, Prince of Peace.
ISAIAH 9:6

The scripture above gives some of the names of Jesus, and if you google the words "names of God," you'll find lists of scriptures pointing you to where you can find many more names used for God. Focusing on these names can be so powerful as we become aware of different aspects of our amazing God and the ways He cares for us.

Here are just a few:

- Elohim means Creator God.
- Adonai means Master over All.
- El Elyon means Most High God.
- Jehovah Jireh means The Lord Will Provide.

With your family or by yourself, you could do a cool prayer project of researching and writing down the many names of God used in the Bible. Then study and use those names as you pray! For example:

Dear Elohim, my Creator God, You are Adonai,
Master over All, including being Master over my life
and every challenge I face. You care about all my needs
because You are Jehovah Jireh and You will always
provide! Thank You, El Elyon, the Most High God! Amen.

❧ HELP FOR THE HELPLESS ❧

Religion that is pure and good before God the Father is to help children who have no parents and to care for women whose husbands have died who have troubles.
JAMES 1:27

As a kid you might struggle to know exactly what you can do to help the most helpless in our world, but keep asking God and He will show you. Maybe there's a canned food drive at school or in your community you can give to. Your church probably has several ministries it contributes to and ways kids can help. Sort through your clothes and toys that you don't use anymore that are still in good shape and donate them to shelters. If you know a family who has adopted or does foster care, ask them how you can help. Pray with your parents about whether adoption or foster care is an option for your family. Find a center that helps moms and babies and see if you can help clean or sort items. And keep praying and praying that God will raise up leaders and organizers who truly love and obey Him and want to protect and provide for the most helpless in our world.

Dear God, show me my part in helping the most helpless among us who are all created in Your image and dearly loved by You! Amen.

☙ prayer for good friends ❧

*Two are better than one, because they have
good pay for their work. For if one of them falls,
the other can help him up. But it is hard for the
one who falls when there is no one to lift him up.*
ECCLESIASTES 4:9–10

Whether you like to have a lot of friends or you're happy
to have just one or two, you need good friends who encourage you, especially who encourage you to love and obey
God. The right kinds of friends are such a blessing. They are
iron sharpening iron as Proverbs 27:17 says, which means
good friends keep helping each other be and do their best.

If you don't already have friends who love and follow
Jesus like you do, ask God to bring them to you. He will,
though it might take some time. I've learned that sometimes
He wants us to grow closer to Him first through prayer and
His Word before He blesses us with a new friend. And if
you're already blessed with good Christian friends, thank
God and ask Him to keep growing your good friendships!

*Dear God, thank You that You want to
bless us with wonderful friends! Amen.*

❧ More Prayer for Friends ❧

Don't fool yourselves. Bad friends will destroy you.
1 CORINTHIANS 15:33 CEV

While the Bible encourages you to have good friends, it also warns against having bad friends, like 1 Corinthians 15:33 says. These scriptures caution against bad friends too:

- "Wise friends make you wise, but you hurt yourself by going around with fools" (Proverbs 13:20 CEV).
- "Don't befriend angry people or associate with hot-tempered people, or you will learn to be like them and endanger your soul" (Proverbs 22:24–25 NLT).

If you find yourself in some bad friendships, with kids who are encouraging you to get into trouble and move far away from obeying God, you will need courage to get out of those friendships. But you absolutely need to. Ask your parents or a trusted grown-up for help and advice, and believe that God will help you be brave if you ask and depend on Him. And then be ready, knowing that those friends might not like your choices. If they treat you badly, hold on to this truth: "God blesses you when people mock you and persecute you and lie about you and say all sorts of evil things against you because you are my followers. Be happy about it! Be very glad! For a great reward awaits you in heaven" (Matthew 5:11–12 NLT).

*Dear God, please help me to be wise about friendships
and to have courage to end friendships that keep
me from staying close to You. Amen.*

❖ pray and provide for the needy ❖

*He who shows kindness to a poor man gives to the Lord
and He will pay him in return for his good act.*
PROVERBS 19:17

You've probably encountered homeless and needy people, maybe when you've visited a big city or even in smaller towns at intersections where needy people often stand with cardboard signs to beg for food and money. My heart aches for each of these people, and only God knows exactly how they got to this point and exactly what they need. You can pray for God to give them the shelter and provisions they need, and you can ask God what He wants *you* to do. Talk to your parents about what they would allow you to do to help and how you can help as a family. Maybe you'll want to put together blessing bags full of snacks and water bottles and a Bible plus things like soap and deodorant and socks to pass out when you see a needy person on the streets. Maybe you can volunteer at a shelter. Find out what your church does to help the needy in your community and join in! Always you can keep asking God to give you compassion and wisdom to come up with good ways to help the needy people around you—and then be ready to obey!

*Dear God, thank You for my blessings. Help me to
share them with those who have so little. Amen.*

❊ THROUGH EVERYTHING GOD HAS MADE ❊

*For ever since the world was created, people have seen the
earth and sky. Through everything God made, they can clearly
see his invisible qualities—his eternal power and divine nature.
So they have no excuse for not knowing God.*
ROMANS 1:20 NLT

We like to watch some popular science and nature shows
and documentaries. The way God created our world is so
cool! But it's sad how *un*popular it is to give God credit as
Creator. When we watch these shows, we try to remember
to pray for the people who make the shows and participate
in them. We pray that they will recognize that nothing in our
world just happened—it's all part of a wonderful design by
our amazing Designer, the one true God! And we pray that
they would believe in the one true God and accept Jesus
Christ as their Savior.

Anyone you know who helps teach you at school or
helps take care of you, like doctors and nurses, might have
tremendous knowledge of God's wonderful creation and
the scientific world without actually acknowledging God as
Creator and Savior. So as you interact with these people,
pray that their eyes would be opened to our amazing God!

*Dear God, You have made Yourself known through
every awesome thing and person You have created.
Please help more and more people to see that
truth and believe in You! Amen.*

❋ Fake Show-offs ❋

"Two men went to the Temple to pray. One was a Pharisee, and the other was a despised tax collector. The Pharisee stood by himself and prayed this prayer: 'I thank you, God, that I am not like other people—cheaters, sinners, adulterers. I'm certainly not like that tax collector! I fast twice a week, and I give you a tenth of my income.' But the tax collector stood at a distance and dared not even lift his eyes to heaven as he prayed. Instead, he beat his chest in sorrow, saying, 'O God, be merciful to me, for I am a sinner.' I tell you, this sinner, not the Pharisee, returned home justified before God. For those who exalt themselves will be humbled, and those who humble themselves will be exalted."
Luke 18:10–14 NLT

The Pharisees in the Bible were the rich and snobby religious leaders who were prideful and loved to act like they were better than others. But they were fakes. The above passage from Luke 18 shows that being show-offs didn't reward them at all. It was the humble tax collector who quickly became right with God because he admitted he was a sinner.

Dear God, I don't ever want to be fake and arrogant toward people like the Pharisees were. Help me to be confident and sincere in who You made me to be, and help me to confidently share Your truth with others. Amen.

❧ Pray To Be Humble ❧

Pride ends in humiliation, while humility brings honor.
PROVERBS 29:23 NLT

God's Word talks a lot about not being proud but instead being humble, but what does that mean exactly? It means not thinking of yourself as better than other people. It means being teachable, knowing you can always keep learning from others and never trying to be a know-it-all. It doesn't mean you can't have any confidence or be happy with your accomplishments, but as a humble Christian, you'll place your confidence in God's work within you, recognizing that He alone gives you the ability to accomplish any good thing!

Read and remember these scriptures, and pray for God to keep your heart humble before Him.

- "The heart of a man is proud before he is destroyed, but having no pride goes before honor" (Proverbs 18:12).
- "So humble yourselves under the mighty power of God, and at the right time he will lift you up in honor" (1 Peter 5:6 NLT).

Dear God, I want to be humble and teachable and give You credit for everything in a world where that's not usually the cool thing to be and do. Please help me. I want to make You happy and trust that You bless and reward and lift me up when I depend completely on You! Amen.

❋ BE ABLE TO LAUGH ❋

Live and work without pride. Be gentle and kind. Do not be hard on others. Let love keep you from doing that.
EPHESIANS 4:2

One way you know you might have too much pride and need more humility is if you can never laugh at yourself. Ephesians 4:2 says not to be hard on others—and so you shouldn't be hard on yourself either! Every single one of us is going to make silly mistakes. Or do clumsy things. Or say something dumb we thought might be funny, but then it totally wasn't. I've done so many of these things I could never keep track of them all. If I have too much pride, I might never be able to get past them or show my face around the people who witnessed them. But if I choose to act humbly and laugh it off and apologize if needed, I can move on, knowing that I am fully loved and forgiven by God and my identity and confidence are in Him.

So pray for God to give you a good sense of humor in those moments when you need to humbly laugh at yourself and move on. His Word says, "A cheerful heart is good medicine, but a broken spirit saps a person's strength" (Proverbs 17:22 NLT). Life's mistakes and embarrassing moments are bound to happen, but you never have to let them break your spirit!

Dear God, help me to be humble enough to laugh at myself and move on from mistakes and embarrassing moments, trusting that I am fully loved and cared for by You! Amen.

❧ Pray to Learn from Mistakes ❧

Pride leads to disgrace, but with humility comes wisdom.
PROVERBS 11:2 NLT

Another way to be a humble person without pride is to be grateful for mistakes because of what they can teach you. Together with a group of young dancers, Jodi and Lilly recently helped lead worship through dance at our church on a Sunday morning, and a lot of people were in attendance. When Lilly made a small mistake in the dance, at first she felt so embarrassed. But she didn't let it stop her from dancing and worshipping. She kept going, with a beaming smile on her face and with arms and legs and body moving in wonderful praise to our amazing God!

What if after she messed up she instantly ran off the stage in embarrassment? That would have been super distracting to the whole worship time. So choosing to move on from the little mistake and focus on going forward doing her best—instead of running away—was definitely the right decision. And even though she cried a few tears afterward to her dance leader and to me, she learned what a good thing it is not to let embarrassing mistakes crush your spirit or stop you from worshipping or doing what God has planned for you. Instead, you can be humble, learn from your mistakes, and keep living, dancing, loving, and bringing God glory!

Dear God, I constantly need to pray for Your help to be humble, to admit mistakes, and to be willing to learn from mistakes. Teach me the lessons that You want me to learn when I mess up. Thank You so much for always loving me, no matter what. Amen.

❄ OUR DAILY FIGHT ❄

*Our fight is not with people. It is against the leaders
and the powers and the spirits of darkness in this world.
It is against the demon world that works in the heavens.
Because of this, put on all the things God gives you to fight
with. Then you will be able to stand in that sinful day. When
it is all over, you will still be standing. So stand up and do not
be moved. Wear a belt of truth around your body. Wear a piece
of iron over your chest which is being right with God. Wear shoes
on your feet which are the Good News of peace. Most important
of all, you need a covering of faith in front of you. This is to
put out the fire-arrows of the devil. The covering for your head
is that you have been saved from the punishment of sin.
Take the sword of the Spirit which is the Word of God.*
EPHESIANS 6:12–17

Every day each of us should wake up remembering we're in
the middle of a fight. That doesn't need to scare us because
God never, ever leaves us. He wants us to fight hard and
stand firm against evil in the world. We do this by putting on
and using all the armor God has given us like the scripture
above tells us.

*Dear God, help me to be on guard each day in
the fight against evil in this world. I want to keep
standing strong for You! Help others to see my faith
in You and want to join in fighting sin and evil. Amen.*

❊ WORSHIP WITH SONG AND PRAYER ❊

*Come, let us sing with joy to the Lord. Let us sing loud
with joy to the rock Who saves us. Let us come before
Him giving thanks. Let us make a sound of joy to Him with
songs. For the Lord is a great God, and a great King above
all gods. The deep places of the earth are in His hand. And
the tops of the mountains belong to Him. The sea is His,
for He made it. And His hands made the dry land. Come,
let us bow down in worship. Let us get down on our knees
before the Lord Who made us. For He is our God.*
PSALM 95:1–7

Do you have favorite worship songs that you especially love?
Awesome if you do! I hope you stop to really focus on the
lyrics sometimes. You could even write them down in your
prayer journal if you're keeping one. Think about the lyrics
and make them both a song and a prayer to God. And even
during times when you're not able to listen to music, ask
God to help the words and tune stick in your mind and let
your mind go to them when you're needing encouragement
and a boost in your faith.

*Dear God, I want songs of praise to
You to fill my mind all the time! Amen.*

❊ STICKY SCRIPTURE ❊

I think about your orders and study your ways. I enjoy obeying
your demands. And I will not forget your word. Do good to me,
your servant, so I can live, so I can obey your word. Open my
eyes to see the wonderful things in your teachings.
PSALM 119:15–18 ICB

Worship songs are great to have stuck in your head, and
even better are the exact words of scripture. And you can
sing them as songs too, of course! Ask God to help scripture
be sticky in your mind when you hear it and read it. It's a
prayer He loves to answer, and so often He'll bring to mind
exactly what you need in encouragement and truth at just
the right moment. His Word is how He wants to guide you
and teach you, and He is so happy when you listen and obey!
Romans 15:4 says, "Everything that was written in the Holy
Writings long ago was written to teach us. By not giving up,
God's Word gives us strength and hope."

Dear God, as I read and listen to and learn
Your Word, please make the scriptures extra sticky
in my mind. I never want them to get out! Amen.

❋ Special Gifts ❋

We all have different gifts that God has given to us by His loving-favor. We are to use them. If someone has the gift of preaching the Good News, he should preach. He should use the faith God has given him. If someone has the gift of helping others, then he should help. If someone has the gift of teaching, he should teach. If someone has the gift of speaking words of comfort and help, he should speak. If someone has the gift of sharing what he has, he should give from a willing heart. If someone has the gift of leading other people, he should lead them. If someone has the gift of showing kindness to others, he should be happy as he does it.
Romans 12:6–8

God has given you special gifts and talents that He wants you to use to help spread His love and bring Him praise! Maybe you have already figured out what some of those gifts are, and you might discover more as you're growing up. Pray for God to give you confidence in the gifts He has given you and ask Him for opportunities to share them well!

Dear God, help me to know my special gifts You've created me with. Show me how You want me to use them. May they point many people to knowing and loving You! Amen.

❧ prayer for contentment ❧

I have learned to be happy with whatever I have. I know how to get along with little and how to live when I have much. I have learned the secret of being happy at all times. If I am full of food and have all I need, I am happy. If I am hungry and need more, I am happy. I can do all things because Christ gives me the strength.
PHILIPPIANS 4:11–13

In his letter to the Philippians, the apostle Paul teaches us a wonderful thing to pray for and tells us how to have it—contentment. In a world with such cool stuff plus the internet that tells us all about it instantly, we often struggle to be content with the life we've been given. It's easy to look at other people's stuff and what they do and where they go on vacation and want all of it instead of or in addition to the good things we already have. We have to pray hard against envy and greed and remember like Paul how to be happy and content. We simply have to remember that we can do all things through Christ who gives us strength. Because He helps us, we can be happy and endure when we have too little and we can be happy and give thanks when we have plenty. Jesus gives us strength no matter what, and trusting in Him is where real contentment comes from!

Dear God, please help me to be content with whatever You decide to bless me with and to trust in Your strength and the ways You provide, no matter what I have or don't have. Amen.

❧ Best Use of Time ❧

So be careful how you live. Live as men who are wise and not foolish. Make the best use of your time. These are sinful days.
EPHESIANS 5:15–16

It's super easy to get distracted or to be lazy about doing the good work God has for us to do. What are the things that tempt you away from doing the things you should be doing (like time with God, schoolwork, chores around the house, etc.)? TV? Video games? Social media? Those things aren't necessarily all bad, but we need to pray and have discipline so they don't get in the way of what's most important in our lives. And what's most important in our lives should be what Jesus said the greatest command is:

> " 'You must love the Lord your God with all your heart and with all your soul and with all your mind.' This is the first and greatest of the Laws. The second is like it, 'You must love your neighbor as you love yourself.' All the Laws and the writings of the early preachers depend on these two most important Laws." (Matthew 22:37–40)

And then we keep asking Him to show us how to live carefully and wisely, making the best use of our time and using our gifts to glorify Him in all the things He has planned for us to do.

....

Dear God, help me to keep Your great commandments first in my life—loving You completely and loving others as myself. Then help me to manage my time wisely to bring the most glory to You! Amen.

❧ Pour Out Your Heart ❧

*As we have suffered much for Christ and have
shared in His pain, we also share His great comfort.*
2 CORINTHIANS 1:5

Think about a time when you've felt rejected. Maybe someone you thought was a good friend excluded you and hurt you and ended the friendship. Maybe you tried out for a school play, positive you'd get a great role, but then didn't get any part at all.

In hurtful, confusing times like these, pour out your heart to God in prayer. He wants to pull you close and comfort you and remind you that Jesus knows exactly what it's like to feel rejected. He knows and He cares. When you share with Him in suffering, you are bonding with Him, and He's developing your faith and your character and also storing up rewards for you in heaven.

So keep trusting and loving our Savior and keep praying, no matter what rejection and suffering you go through. He is good through it all, and He is working to make all things right!

*Dear Jesus, when I feel rejected, remind me how
rejected You were—so rejected that people beat You
and then killed You on the cross. But that sure wasn't
the end. In Your rejection and suffering God was working
to save the world. Remind me that You are working in
ways I don't know yet when I am rejected and suffering
too. Please comfort me and strengthen my faith
as You work behind the scenes! Amen.*

❧ JONAH'S PRAYER ❧

The Lord sent a big fish to swallow Jonah.
JONAH 1:17

What's the worst, most bizarre way you can think of that your parents might discipline you for disobedience? I'm guessing Jonah in the Bible never imagined he'd wind up in the belly of a giant fish! But he did end up there because he didn't obey God. And inside that fish, he prayed:

> *"I called out to the Lord because of my trouble, and He answered me. I cried for help from the place of the dead, and You heard my voice. You threw me into the deep waters, to the very bottom of the sea. . . . But You have brought me up from the grave, O Lord my God. While I was losing all my strength, I remembered the Lord. And my prayer came to You, into Your holy house. Those who worship false gods have given up their faith in You. But I will give gifts in worship to You with a thankful voice. I will give You what I have promised. The Lord is the One Who saves."*
> *Then the Lord spoke to the fish, and it spit Jonah out onto the dry land. (Jonah 2:2–3, 6–10)*

Dear God, help me to learn from Jonah that there are always negative consequences for disobeying You. Thank You, though, that You still love and care for Your people when they make mistakes, and You hear and answer their cries for help when they repent and want to obey You again. Amen.

❧ prayer when grieving ❧

O Lord my God, I cried to You
for help and You healed me.
PSALM 30:2

If someone you love has ever died very suddenly, you might know, like we do, that it's an awful shock to lose someone with zero warning. Losing a loved one in any kind of way, whether you have a chance to say goodbye or not, is heartbreaking. But we've learned and experienced how God gives extraspecial grace and care when we stay close to Him and let Him heal our broken hearts—even when we don't fully understand Him. We stayed close to Him through His Word and through prayer, crying out to Him with all our grieving emotions, including sadness, anger, fear, and confusion. And we have been amazed at how He has comforted and provided in many different ways.

If you are grieving the loss of a loved one, keep crying out to God and reading His Word. Tell Him everything you are feeling, even the angry and confused feelings, and ask for His help. Search His Word and let Him show you how He will heal your heart, giving you His love through many different sources and people.

Dear God, please hold me extra close when I am grieving
and missing a loved one. I don't understand, but I don't
want to turn away from You. Please comfort me and
heal my heart and grow my faith in You. Amen.

A Test for God?

"Bring to the storehouse a tenth of what you gain. Then there will be food in my house. Test me in this," says the Lord of heaven's armies. "I will open the windows of heaven for you. I will pour out more blessings than you have room for."
MALACHI 3:10 ICB

You don't normally think of getting to give your teacher a test, do you? Well, God is the greatest teacher of all, and there is one way He actually wants us to give Him a test! It's by seeing how much He gives to us in return when we choose to be cheerful givers to Him. Start while you are young and make a habit your whole life of giving at least one-tenth of the money you earn back to God. Remember, any ability you have to work comes from God anyway, and simply giving 10 percent of it is a wonderful way to thank Him. You get to keep 90 percent! This giving is called tithing. How do you tithe money to God? By giving to churches and ministries that teach His Word and serve and care for people like Jesus did, in His great name. And giving to others as you see they have needs. Time and time again, God will bless you for doing so. It's not always in terms of money that He will give back to you (though sometimes it is) but also in ways like special opportunities and close relationships and good health and unexpected treats and on and on! Test Him and see, praying for Him to show you as you do.

Dear God, show me how much You love to give to me when I love to give to You! Amen.

❧ CHOOSE WITH CARE ❧

Test everything and do not let good things get away from you.
Keep away from everything that even looks like sin.
1 THESSALONIANS 5:21–22

We sure have a lot of options in movies, TV, music, and social media these days. And so we have all the more reason to pray for wisdom about what we watch, listen to, read, and participate in on the internet. We should strive to be able to say, like David did in Psalm 101:1–5 (NLT),

> *I will sing of your love and justice, LORD. I will praise you with songs. I will be careful to live a blameless life—when will you come to help me? I will lead a life of integrity in my own home. I will refuse to look at anything vile and vulgar. I hate all who deal crookedly; I will have nothing to do with them. I will reject perverse ideas and stay away from every evil. I will not tolerate people who slander their neighbors. I will not endure conceit and pride.*

> *Dear God, please help me as I make media and social media choices. Sometimes the options seem so out of control for girls my age, and it's sure not a popular choice to be careful! But I love You, and I want to stay away from anything that causes me to sin and disappoint You. Amen.*

☀ LIGHTHOUSE LESSON ☀

This is the day that the Lord has made.
Let us be full of joy and be glad in it.
PSALM 118:24

Once while in Florida, we were all excited to climb up the steep stairs inside a historic lighthouse and see the beautiful views from the top. But when we got there, we learned Lilly wasn't quite tall enough to be allowed to climb up. We were all bummed we were unable to go together, Lilly especially! Maybe you've had something like this happen to you.

Sometimes life is like that. There are age limits and rules to follow that we might not fully agree with or understand and we might be disappointed by. But we have a choice how we respond in those frustrating situations. We can choose to pout and be grumpy, or we can choose to have a good attitude. The lighthouse situation was hard for Lilly at first, but soon she was choosing to have a good attitude and also to be grateful for the blessing that day—she was given a free pass to come back and climb the lighthouse in a year or so when tall enough. We haven't had a chance to get back there and use that pass yet, so she still has that blessing to look forward to!

Dear God, please help me when I need to accept limits and rules that I don't like or don't understand. Help me to choose a good attitude even when I'm frustrated. Amen.

❧ HEAD IN THE CLOUDS ❧

Keep your minds thinking about things in heaven.
COLOSSIANS 3:2

God has wonderful plans for each of our lives on earth! Ephesians 2:10 (ICB) says, "In Christ Jesus, God made us new people so that we would do good works. God had planned in advance those good works for us. He had planned for us to live our lives doing them." But God doesn't want us to get too attached to our lives here on earth because they are not our forever lives with Him in heaven. First John 2:15–17 (NLT) says, "Do not love this world nor the things it offers you, for when you love the world, you do not have the love of the Father in you. For the world offers only a craving for physical pleasure, a craving for everything we see, and pride in our achievements and possessions. These are not from the Father, but are from this world. And this world is fading away, along with everything that people crave. But anyone who does what pleases God will live forever."

We need to keep the perspective of finding joy and purpose in the good plans for which God has created us while remembering that our life on earth is temporary and our forever home is in heaven.

Dear God, thank You for the good plans You created me for here on earth. Help me to walk closely with You and do them for Your glory. And thank You that someday I will live forever in perfect heaven! Amen.

❋ JOB'S PRAYER OF PRAISE ❋

There was a man in the land of Uz whose name was Job.
That man was without blame. He was right and good,
he feared God, and turned away from sin.
JOB 1:1

Job's faith in God was tested in such an incredibly difficult way. It's hard to even imagine the pain and sorrow he endured. Yet after losing so much, including his livestock, his servants, and all his children, "Job stood up and tore his clothing and cut the hair from his head. And he fell to the ground and worshiped. He said, 'Without clothing I was born from my mother, and without clothing I will return. The Lord gave and the Lord has taken away. Praise the name of the Lord.' In all this Job did not sin or blame God" (Job 1:20–22).

We can follow Job's example in this prayer, and no matter what God gives to us or takes away from our lives, we can trust and worship God through it all.

Dear God, help me to have faith and endurance like Job,
so that no matter what hard things I have to go through,
I will choose to trust and praise You. Amen.

❄ Job's Prayer of Repentance ❄

"He who speaks strong words against God, let him answer."
Job 40:2

If you read the whole book of Job, you will find that as it goes on, Job was tested even more and he did not continue to praise God through it all. In fact, he had quite angry words for a while. But in the end, after God reminded Job of His greatness and goodness, Job cried out in repentance, telling God how sorry he was:

> *"I know that You can do all things. Nothing can put a stop to Your plans. 'Who is this that hides words of wisdom without much learning?' I have said things that I did not understand, things too great for me, which I did not know. 'Hear now, and I will speak. I will ask you, and you answer Me.' I had heard of You only by the hearing of the ear, but now my eye sees You. So I hate the things that I have said. And I put dust and ashes on myself to show how sorry I am."*
> (Job 42:2–6)

We need to learn from Job that when we cry out to God with angry words, we should stop and realize God's power and love and control over all things, in ways we cannot understand. And we need to say we are sorry for disrespecting God. After Job repented, God blessed him again even more than he had been blessed in the first place!

....

*Dear God, help me to learn from Job that
if I speak in anger to You, I need to say I'm
sorry and continue to trust in You. Amen.*

☀ our unchanging god ☀

*Jesus Christ is the same yesterday
and today and forever.*
HEBREWS 13:8

We've had a whole lot of change in our lives in the last few years, and it hasn't always been easy. Can you think of a time when you've experienced major change? What were your thoughts and emotions and prayers like during that time?

Nothing in life will always stay the same, and that's why we can be so thankful that God gave us Jesus, who is always dependable and always the same—yesterday, today, and forever! Psalm 102:25–27 says of God, "You made the earth in the beginning. You made the heavens with Your hands. They will be destroyed but You will always live. They will all become old as clothing becomes old. You will change them like a coat. And they will be changed, but You are always the same. Your years will never end."

Our all-powerful God is never going to let us down. So lean on Him and ask Him to hold you steady when life seems to swirl around you with new and unanticipated circumstances. Talk to Him about every joy and sorrow and stress.

*Dear God, thank You for never changing or letting
me down through all life's ups and downs! Amen.*

❧ GOOD GIFTS ❧

*"You fathers—if your children ask for a fish, do you give them
a snake instead? Or if they ask for an egg, do you give them a
scorpion? Of course not! So if you sinful people know how to give
good gifts to your children, how much more will your heavenly
Father give the Holy Spirit to those who ask him."*
LUKE 11:11–13 NLT

Have you ever played with Bunch O Balloons, the kind of
water balloons attached together so you can fill up a whole
bunch at once? Jodi and Lilly have fallen in love with those
this summer as we've been writing this book. They love to
take them on the trampoline and slip and splash while they
jump. Their dad went to the store the other night and surprised them by bringing home some more because they love
them so much. And then, as a bonus surprise, the package
had a contest code and we won some *more* Bunch O Balloons that will come in the mail sometime soon.

This made me think of the scripture in Luke 11. Great
dads do love to surprise their children with good gifts. Moms
do too! And our heavenly Daddy loves it so much more than
earthly parents do. So it's totally okay to ask your heavenly
Father for good gifts!

*Dear God, thank You so much for wanting to
bless me with good gifts. I am so grateful! Amen.*

❊ Anna, a Woman of Prayer ❊

Anna was a woman who spoke God's Word. She was the daughter of Phanuel of the family group of Asher. Anna was many years old. She had lived with her husband seven years after she was married. Her husband had died and she had lived without a husband eighty-four years. Yet she did not go away from the house of God. She served God day and night, praying and going without food so she could pray better. At that time she came and gave thanks to God. She told the people in Jerusalem about Jesus. They were looking for the One to save them from the punishment of their sins and to set them free.
Luke 2:36–38

We hope you like to learn about historical women. Even though they lived so long ago, the women of the Bible who loved God should still inspire us today! One of these is Anna, a woman you can look up to and model your life after. She had lost her husband yet wanted to serve God wholeheartedly and pray all the time. She was delighted when Jesus was born and praised God because she knew Jesus would be our Savior.

....

Dear God, help me to be like Anna, serving You no matter what and wanting to pray more and more to grow ever closer to You. Amen.

❖ prayer for your country ❖

Pray for kings and all others who are in power over us so we might live quiet God-like lives in peace. It is good when you pray like this. It pleases God Who is the One Who saves.
1 TIMOTHY 2:2–3

You might hear your parents or other grown-ups talking a lot about politics or hear about politics at school. It can be confusing and frustrating, for sure, to understand what's going on and to discern which politicians might be good leaders for our nation. Since you're a kid and can't vote, you might think there's nothing you can do, but there is always something. You can pray, of course! Pray for the leaders of our nation, the president and vice president and their families and all elected officials in federal, state, and local government and their families too. Praying for so many people might seem overwhelming, but you could think of the American flag as a reminder. Every time you see it, pray something like this:

Dear God, please bless our nation according to Your will. Help our leaders want to acknowledge and honor You. Please give them Your wisdom to govern well. May each of them know You as the one true God and Savior. Please protect our nation and protect our freedom to worship You, and help us to use that freedom to spread Your truth and love. Amen.

❧ prayer for the world ❧

"Be still, and know that I am God! I will be honored by every nation. I will be honored throughout the world."
PSALM 46:10 NLT

You can pray specifically for each state in your country too. Put a map on a wall somewhere in your house; use it as a visual to remind you to pray, and pick a state to pray for each day. You could also make a chart listing people you know in each state and remember them in extraspecial prayer the same day you pray for their state.

And don't just stop there. God loves everyone everywhere in the whole world, not just our nation. So get a globe and start praying for every person in every country and for nations to honor the one true God and to do His will according to His Word.

. . . .

Dear God, You love all people of all nations, and You want them to honor You and trust Jesus as Savior so You can give them eternal life. You are such a good and loving heavenly Father. Help me to remember to pray for all people everywhere! Amen.

❧ BreaD OF LIFE ❧

*Jesus said, "I tell you the truth, Moses didn't give you
bread from heaven. My Father did. And now he offers you the
true bread from heaven. The true bread of God is the one
who comes down from heaven and gives life to the world."
"Sir," they said, "give us that bread every day." Jesus replied,
"I am the bread of life. Whoever comes to me will never be
hungry again. Whoever believes in me will never be thirsty."*
JOHN 6:32–35 NLT

Think about things in your home you can't imagine living
without. Indoor plumbing? Electricity? Air-conditioning?
Wi-Fi? We are very blessed with modern conveniences in
this day and age! But our most basic daily needs for life
are food and water, right? We couldn't survive long without them. So does Jesus say in this scripture that He ex-
pects us to believe in Him and never eat food or drink
water again? No, but Jesus does want us to trust in Him as
the One who provides for all our needs. *He* is actually our
most basic need for life because He is the giver of life—
eternal life!

*Dear Jesus, thank You for being the giver of life!
I trust in You, and You are everything I need. Amen.*

❧ PRAY THE PSALMS ❧

The Lord is right and good in all His ways, and kind in all His works. The Lord is near to all who call on Him, to all who call on Him in truth. He will fill the desire of those who fear Him. He will also hear their cry and will save them. The Lord takes care of all who love Him. But He will destroy all the sinful. My mouth will speak the praise of the Lord. And all flesh will honor His holy name forever and ever.
PSALM 145:17–21

Anytime you open up the book of Psalms, you can read and pray and be encouraged by all the poetic passages that are prayers and praises to God. They are full of honest emotion as the writers pour out their hearts to God, and they can inspire you to do the same. There is nothing you need to hide from God. If you have sin in your life, confess it to Him and make it right. If you are hurting, tell God and let Him comfort you. If you are in need or a loved one is, ask God for His help. If you are scared, let God remind you of His power and protection. If you are full of gratitude and praise, tell Him again and again!

Dear God, help me to remember to turn to the Psalms often and be inspired by honest prayer and praise. Amen.

❧ BOW DOWN ❧

Then Ezra praised the LORD, the great God, and all the
people chanted, "Amen! Amen!" as they lifted their
hands. Then they bowed down and worshiped
the LORD with their faces to the ground.
NEHEMIAH 8:6 NLT

Maybe you've learned to always bow your head, close your
eyes, and fold your hands to pray, and that posture is good
to help you focus on God. But really there is no specific position you have to pray in because you never have to stop
praying to God. You can be sitting or standing or raising your
hands, and you can be anywhere at all when you pray. But
sometimes it's good to position your body in a way that reminds you of God's total greatness and your total respect
for, devotion to, and need for Him.

If you don't already, you can start bowing your head and
kneeling before God beside your bed at night. At our girls'
group at church, we have been so encouraged on Wednes-
days when we spend a little time on our knees to pray and
worship God together, ages kindergarten through fifth
grade plus teen and adult female leaders. What a blessing
to participate in prayer this way, with a full room of girls and
women who want to know and love God better!

Dear God, help me to remember that I can pray
to You anywhere I am, but I also want to remember
to bow and kneel before You at times because I
respect and love You so much. I am so grateful to
be a child of the King of all kings! I worship You, my
Creator, my Savior, and my awesome God! Amen.

☀ Guard Your Heart ☀

Guard your heart above all else,
for it determines the course of your life.
PROVERBS 4:23 NLT

If you've ever gotten a really nasty illness, you probably wanted to figure out what caused it so that hopefully you never have to endure it again, right? Just like we need to be aware of what's going on with our bodies and any aches or illnesses we might have, we need to be aware of our thoughts and emotions and what's causing them, whether good or bad.

If you feel great love for your siblings most of the time, awesome! But if you feel great anger toward them most of the time, not so awesome, right? If you feel sad some of the time, that's understandable. But what if you feel sad *all* the time? Not good! You need to figure out where confusing and overwhelming emotions are coming from and how to communicate about them plus hopefully work out what's causing them. Ask your parents and trusted grown-ups for help and be totally honest about your feelings. And never forget that God knows your heart best of all, and He can help you with everything you feel. Pray to Him and ask Him to give you great wisdom when it comes to your thoughts and emotions and actions and how they all interact.

Dear God, sometimes I have a lot of confusing emotions that I'm not sure what to do with. You know my heart and every thought and feeling even better than I do. Can You please help me sort them out and communicate them well? I also need people like my parents and others who are good at this to help me too. Thank You for caring about every detail of me, God! Amen.

❊ STANDSTILL ❊

On the day the LORD gave the Israelites victory over the Amorites, Joshua prayed to the LORD in front of all the people of Israel. He said, "Let the sun stand still over Gibeon, and the moon over the valley of Aijalon." So the sun stood still and the moon stayed in place until the nation of Israel had defeated its enemies. Is this event not recorded in The Book of Jashar? The sun stayed in the middle of the sky, and it did not set as on a normal day. There has never been a day like this one before or since, when the LORD answered such a prayer. Surely the LORD fought for Israel that day!
JOSHUA 10:12–14 NLT

Amazing! Joshua prayed for the sun and moon to stand still to give extra daylight in order for God's people to win the war against their enemies the Amorites. And God answered in a way He had never done before and has never done again. When you have a huge prayer request, you can think about this story of Joshua and let it build your faith. God is able to command anything in His creation to obey His Word. So surely He is able to help you with every one of your needs, as well as those of your family and friends!

Dear God, please remind me constantly of Your all-powerful ways over all creation! No problem is too big for You! Thank You that I can bring every concern I have to You. Amen.

❧ Demanding Daisy ❧

O LORD, our Lord, your majestic name fills the earth! Your glory is higher than the heavens. . . . When I look at the night sky and see the work of your fingers—the moon and the stars you set in place—what are mere mortals that you should think about them, human beings that you should care for them?

PSALM 8:1, 3–4 NLT

We laugh at our little dog Daisy because pretty much anytime we're in the kitchen, she comes in barking in such a demanding way she seems to be saying, "Give me a treat *now!*" She especially loves little slices of apple, but she'll eat almost anything if we let her.

Do you ever get what you want by demanding things from others? I hope you don't. That's rude and disrespectful. We should never demand things of God either. We should come to Him humbly and with total respect. Don't be like our demanding Daisy to anyone, and especially not to God!

....

Dear God, help me not to be demanding and rude when I ask others for things. Please forgive me and help me make it right when I mess up and do that. And help me never to be demanding of You. I trust that You always want to give me what's best for me, and I humbly ask You to do so. Amen.

❀ Remember ❀

My voice goes up to God, and I will cry out.
My voice goes up to God and He will hear me.
PSALM 77:1

Sometimes God answers our prayers by telling us to *remember* because He wants us to focus on what He has done and how He has provided in the past. In Psalm 77, the psalmist starts out troubled and crying and asking questions and wondering if God has forgotten him. But then his tone changes and he prays, "I will remember the things the Lord has done. Yes, I will remember the powerful works of long ago. I will think of all Your work, and keep in mind all the great things You have done. O God, Your way is holy. What god is great like our God? You are the God Who does great works" (Psalm 77:11–14).

So if you're waiting for an answer to prayer, maybe God would like you to remember as you wait. And rather than worry about your current or future needs, you can fill your mind with praise as you recall how God has worked in the past! Then you'll be building your faith strong for how He's helping you now and how He will continue to help you in the future.

....

Dear God, I never have reason to doubt You
because all I have to do is remember all You have
done in the past. May Your will be done now and in the
future too. I will wait on You and trust in You. Amen.

❧ Questions on Repeat ❧

God has said, "I will never leave you or let you be alone."
HEBREWS 13:5

Once when Lilly was three years old we were at a hotel in Virginia Beach, and she was afraid to go down the short tunnel slide into the pool. She finally did it (with arm floaties securely in place!) but only with her daddy waiting at the bottom to catch her. And before every trip down she had a list of questions she called down the tube to her daddy:

- *"Are you there?"*
- *"Are you ready?"*
- *"Are you sure?"*
- *"Will you catch me?"*
- *"Do you promise?"*

Every. single. time. she asked these five questions in exactly the same way before she would go down the slide, and every single time her daddy assured her the answer to all of them was yes. She must have done this at least twenty times, and it's a sweet memory we will never forget.

We like to think of this story in relation to the way we call on our heavenly Daddy in prayer. He absolutely answers yes to all these questions too, and He won't get tired of answering—even zillions of times! He's always there, always ready to help, always sticking to His promises, always so glad to hear from us in prayer.

Dear God, thank You for loving me so well. Thank You that I can depend on You no matter what my circumstances. Amen.

❈ SUDDENLY SWIMMING ❈

Be strong with the Lord's strength.
EPHESIANS 6:10

During that same trip to Virginia Beach, Jodi had just turned six years old and was trying to overcome some of her own fears, and particularly to swim without arm floaties. I kept encouraging her to take them off, but she didn't want to. Then after a pool break, she went back to the water, got halfway down the slide, and then discovered she had forgotten to put her floaties back on! There was no turning back! She hit the water, which was over her head, and was forced to just start swimming—and she totally did! She was a mix of scared, relieved, and super excited after she climbed the steps out of the pool and came to tell us what had happened.

Sometimes in life we are just unexpectedly thrown into things we think we don't know how to do. Sometimes God lets that happen on purpose so we can get over our fears and to show us He wants us to depend on Him for His help. He is always there, and we can always call on Him in prayer. We might be surprised at what we are capable of with His power working in us!

Dear God, sometimes I find myself unexpectedly thrown into situations where I don't have a clue what to do! Help me to realize how much I can depend on You and Your power in those times. Teach me and strengthen me, please, God! Amen.

❖ GOD'S GREATNESS ❖

God's riches are so great! The things He knows and His wisdom are so deep! No one can understand His thoughts. No one can understand His ways. The Holy Writings say, "Who knows the mind of the Lord? Who is able to tell Him what to do?" "Who has given first to God, that God should pay him back?" Everything comes from Him. His power keeps all things together. All things are made for Him. May He be honored forever. Let it be so.
ROMANS 11:33–36

Keep Romans 11:33–36 in mind every time you pray. God's riches and power and thoughts and ways are so far above and beyond anything you can possibly imagine. So pray big, telling God you know that nothing is impossible for Him to do, yet humbly, asking according to His will. And keep wanting God to grow your faith in Him no matter what His answers to prayer are.

Dear God, remind me to focus on how awesome You are. My mind can't fully understand You, but I want to grow closer to You and honor You. Please strengthen my faith in You and my relationship with You every day of my life. Amen.

❧ safe in God's care ❧

*God is our safe place and our strength. He is always
our help when we are in trouble. So we will not be afraid,
even if the earth is shaken and the mountains fall into
the center of the sea, and even if its waters go wild with
storm and the mountains shake with its action.*
PSALM 46:1–3

How do you feel about thunderstorms? What's the scariest
experience you've had in one? I'm not a big fan because
of all the damage I know they can do. I'm thankful for a
basement to go to when storms are raging outside. Psalm
46:1–3 is a wonderful passage to memorize and recite on
repeat during a scary storm or any kind of disaster or emergency. We are always safe when we are in God's care. He is
our Strength and our Help in times of trouble.

*Dear God, I have nothing to fear because You keep me
safe. Please help me to remember that You are my
safe place, even during the loudest thunderstorms or
worse. Thank You for Your strength and help. Amen.*

❧ Marvelous Masterpiece ❧

*For we are God's masterpiece. He has created
us anew in Christ Jesus, so we can do the
good things he planned for us long ago.*
EPHESIANS 2:10 NLT

I love to talk with Jodi and Lilly as they dream about the many things they might do as grown-ups. And this scripture is one we've memorized and think about as we pray for their futures. God has created each of us as a marvelous masterpiece with good plans for us in mind, so we pray this way—and you can too:

Dear God, thank You for creating me totally unique. Even my fingerprints are unlike those of any other person in the world. That's so cool! I believe You have good plans for me and good works You want me to do, and I believe my life will be best when I'm following those plans and doing those works! Will You please show and guide me every day? Even now while I'm so young, please put desires in my heart and mind that match the things You want me to do. Please help my schoolwork and the activities I choose to prepare me for those things too. Please open doors of opportunity You want me to walk through and close doors You don't want for me. I want to live a life of serving You and following Your will for me. I believe that is the most rewarding kind of life! Amen.

❋ LIFE'S LITTLE JOYS ❋

*Be happy in your hope. Do not give up when trouble comes.
Do not let anything stop you from praying.*
ROMANS 12:12

One of our favorite things about summer is a local hot air balloon festival. There is just something so delightful about seeing a sky full of brightly colored balloons. We'd love to visit New Mexico someday and see the Albuquerque International Balloon Festival, the largest hot air balloon event in the world!

What are some of your favorite simple joys? Jodi and Lilly shared they love spending time with family and our dogs and even just looking at the stars in the night sky.

I hope you have many simple things that bring you joy. A lot of sad and stressful things happen in this life, but God doesn't want us to be defeated by them (Romans 12:21). I believe He gives us little things to delight in to help us through those hard times. And ultimately our joy doesn't depend on the situation we're going through; it depends on whether we know Jesus as Savior. With Him as our source of joy, we never run out of it!

....

*Dear God, all my hope is in You, and all my joy
comes from You! Thank You for all the little
joys of life until one day we have constant,
perfect joy forever in heaven with You! Amen.*

❊ more joy and hope ❊

*Your faith will bring thanks and shining-greatness and honor
to Jesus Christ when He comes again. You have never seen
Him but you love Him. You cannot see Him now but you are
putting your trust in Him. And you have joy so great that
words cannot tell about it. You will get what your faith is
looking for, which is to be saved from the punishment of sin.*
1 Peter 1:7–9

The Bible talks a lot about real joy that comes from knowing
God and trusting Jesus as Savior. If you're ever feeling blue
and need some extra reminders about joy, read and hold on
to these scriptures:

- "Be full of joy always because you belong to the
  Lord. Again I say, be full of joy!" (Philippians 4:4).
- "You will show me the way of life. Being with You is
  to be full of joy. In Your right hand there is happiness
  forever" (Psalm 16:11).
- "If you obey My teaching, you will live in My love.
  In this way, I have obeyed My Father's teaching
  and live in His love. I have told you these things
  so My joy may be in you and your joy may be full"
  (John 15:10–11).

*Dear God, when I'm feeling down, please remind
me of the many reasons I have to be full of
joy—most of all because of You! Amen.*

❊ BUILDING UP ❊

But you, dear friends, must build each other up in your most
holy faith, pray in the power of the Holy Spirit, and await the
mercy of our Lord Jesus Christ, who will bring you eternal life.
In this way, you will keep yourselves safe in God's love.
JUDE 1:20–21 NLT

If you build a Lego tower with just a single skinny column of bricks, you can build it really tall, right? But it's not very strong and topples easily. But if you build it wide with more bricks at the bottom and with supporting bricks as you build up, you can have a tower that is both strong and tall! You can think of prayer as a major source of strength and support as you build the tower of your life as a follower of Jesus. You want your life in Him to be strong and not easily toppled! Spending time in God's Word, learning at a Bible-teaching church, serving God by serving others, and having fellowship with other Christians are good sources of strength and support for your life of following Jesus. If these are all part of your life now and continue as you grow up, just think how strong and tall for God you can be as a grown-up!

Dear God, I want to be built up strong in
my faith in You. Help me to pray and learn
and serve You all of my days! Amen.

❀ conversation starters ❀

Is anyone among you suffering? He should pray. Is anyone happy?
He should sing songs of thanks to God.
JAMES 5:13

Sometimes we play a little "High Low" conversation game at bedtime where we share our best part of the day, the high, and our worst part of the day, the low. Sometimes we get a little carried away also sharing our most boring part and funniest part and stinkiest part and scariest part and on and on, until I realize Jodi and Lilly are really just trying to delay going to sleep. Ha!

But truly it's so good to share about our days with each other. These conversation starters can also be great prayer starters. Invite God into every conversation, knowing He's already constantly present with you anyway and loves to be welcome. When you're sharing about the different events of the day and how they made you feel, give any worries and fears and needs to God and praise Him for all the good things. He cares about every high and every low and everything in between.

Dear God, please help me to remember Your constant
presence with me. I welcome You into every part of my life, into
every conversation. I love You and need You! Amen.

❧ Real Love ❧

*And now we have these three: faith and hope
and love, but the greatest of these is love.*
1 CORINTHIANS 13:13

Our world has a lot of wrong ideas about what love is, so we need God's instructions about love more than anything else! He *is* love, 1 John 4:8 tells us. All real love flows from Him and His Word. None of us would know anything about love if not for God!

First Corinthians 13 teaches us that real love "does not give up. Love is kind. Love is not jealous. Love does not put itself up as being important. Love has no pride. Love does not do the wrong thing. Love never thinks of itself. Love does not get angry. Love does not remember the suffering that comes from being hurt by someone. Love is not happy with sin. Love is happy with the truth. Love takes everything that comes without giving up. Love believes all things. Love hopes for all things. Love keeps on in all things. Love never comes to an end" (verses 4–8).

*Dear God, help me to learn and live by what You say
about real love—because You are real love! Amen.*

❧ No Complaints ❧

Do everything without complaining and arguing.
PHILIPPIANS 2:14 NLT

When I asked Jodi and Lilly to name their least favorite thing to do around the house, Jodi said sweeping the floor and Lilly said cleaning her room. I'm guessing you have some least favorite chores too. I know I sure do! It's easy to complain about them, but God's Word says not to complain about anything! And it really just makes the job all the worse to get done (and maybe even take longer, and who wants that?) if we choose a bad attitude while we work.

We sure don't do this perfectly, but we try to make cleanup time a time of praise and prayer. We can put on good worship music and sing while we do our chores. Then our minds focus on God and His love instead of grumpy thoughts wishing our houses would just clean themselves.

Ask God to help you make a habit of pushing negative complaining out of your brain. If complaints never stay in your brain, they can never move to your mouth or spread into a really bad attitude.

....

Dear God, I don't want to be a complainer. I need Your help all the time to replace complaining with good and positive thoughts, especially praise and worship to You! Amen.

❧ communication, not complaints ❧

*"If your brother sins against you, go and tell him
what he did without other people hearing it."*
MATTHEW 18:15

Sometimes people who just love to have everything peaceful can take a verse like Philippians 2:14, which says to do everything without complaining, a little too far. Does it mean don't complain if your friend wants you to give her your homework to copy? Of course not. There are absolutely many times to *not* do things but to stand up and say, "This is not okay."

Complaining should never be confused with communicating and working out conflict. We need to have hard conversations sometimes to help improve relationships and situations. For example, telling your sister you're frustrated with the unfair way she uses your stuff without asking is *not* complaining. You need to talk and work out the situation together, not just keep letting her get away with being selfish and disrespectful toward you. We should pray for God to help us embrace good communication and good conflict. Fear of constructive conflict is one of Satan's tactics to keep people sinning and trying to hold unfair power over each other rather than working toward good relationships and teamwork.

*Dear God, help me to be wise and know the difference
between complaining and good communication.
I want to be able to work out conflict in good
and healthy ways with Your help! Amen.*

❊ No Drama Llamas ❊

God blesses those people who make peace.
MATTHEW 5:9 CEV

We think all the "No Drama Llama" stuff you see in stores these days is pretty cute! Because unless it's the kind of drama like watching a play or a musical, or maybe a close competition like an exciting basketball game down to the last second, drama just for the sake of drama is not cool. We shouldn't love being in conflict and competition with others; instead we should always want good and peaceful relationships, forgiving each other and not gossiping or causing fights.

Yet the Bible says blessed are the peace*makers*, and you can't *make* anything without some work, right? So it takes some working out of disagreements and trouble to make peace sometimes, not just going along with anything to try to keep everyone happy and drama-free. We need so much help and wisdom from God to know how to do this right. Fortunately, God promises us that He loves to give us wisdom (see James 1:5). He totally loves to help us with our problems, so just keep asking!

....

Dear God, help me to be a no-drama llama yet also someone willing to work out conflict and be a peacemaker. I am so grateful for Your wisdom and help. I need You so much! Amen.

❧ Be a God Pleaser ❧

I'm not trying to win the approval of people,
but of God. If pleasing people were my goal,
I would not be Christ's servant.
GALATIANS 1:10 NLT

To want approval means you want to be accepted and found pleasing and good. And it's hard not to want that from people when you desire to have friends and get along well with people. But God's Word shows us we shouldn't be looking for approval from people. We should look for God's approval most of all. If you start praying now while you're young to be a God pleaser and a servant of Jesus, not a people pleaser, you'll help yourself out in so many ways! You won't be so worried what other people think of you. You won't want to give in to peer pressure. You'll be true to the unique, amazing person God designed you to be. You'll follow the awesome plan God has for you and have the most rewarding kind of life! You might not always get this right, because living for God's approval can be hard! But as you pray, God will help you keep your focus on Him, and at the same time He'll be filling your life with the good and loving relationships you need with others.

Dear God, I want to please You! I need Your help to
keep my attention on what You think of me and want
for me, not what others think and want. Please keep
showing me that when my focus is on You, everything
else in my life falls into place exactly like You want,
and that is the very best life! Amen.

❄ Real Girl Power ❄

If Christ keeps giving me his power, I will gladly brag
about how weak I am. Yes, I am glad to be weak or insulted
or mistreated or to have troubles and sufferings, if it is
for Christ. Because when I am weak, I am strong.
2 Corinthians 12:9–10 cev

There's a lot of talk about girl power in our world today, and it's good to want to be a strong girl. But sometimes our world's idea of strong girls is very different from God's will and His ways. To be truly strong, Jodi, Lilly, and I pray for God to help us be strong *in Him*. The Bible actually tells us to be happy about our weaknesses because when we can admit we are weak we can ask God for His power and He will keep giving it! On our own, we could never have greater power than God's, so being filled with God's limitless power is absolutely amazing! He loves to give it, so look at your weakness as a blessing, admit it, and then ask God to make you a mighty strong girl in His power!

Dear God, I admit my many weaknesses and I'm glad
for them because they make me depend on You. Please
fill me with Your awesome power and strength and
make me a truly strong girl. Thank You! Amen.

❧ only one? ❧

*As He was going into one of the towns, ten men with
a bad skin disease came to Him. They stood a little way
off. They called to Him, "Jesus! Teacher! Take pity on us!"
When Jesus saw them, He said, "Go and show yourselves
to the religious leaders." As they went, they were healed.
One of them turned back when he saw he was healed.
He thanked God with a loud voice. He got down on his face
at the feet of Jesus and thanked Him. He was from the
country of Samaria. Jesus asked, "Were there not ten men
who were healed? Where are the other nine? Is this stranger
from another country the only one who turned back to give
thanks to God?" Then Jesus said to him, "Get up and go
on your way. Your trust in God has healed you."*
LUKE 17:12–19

Hopefully you've been learning since you were very small
to be polite and always say please and thank you. But this
account in Luke 17 reminds us how easy it is to forget to say
thank you. These ten men had been miraculously healed by
Jesus. You'd think they would have been almost bursting
with gratitude. Yet only one of them turned back to Jesus
to actually say thank You and worship Him. In whatever ways
God blesses us, we should always want to be like the one
man and not the other nine!

. . . .

*Dear God, please help me never to forget to
give You thanks for all You do for me! I want to
worship and praise You for everything. Amen.*

❧ COUNT THEM UP ❧

Sing in your heart to the Lord. Always give
thanks for all things to God the Father
in the name of our Lord Jesus Christ.
EPHESIANS 5:19–20

To help you be like the one man in Luke 17 and not the other nine, start now to make mental and/or written lists as a way to thank God regularly for your many blessings! Maybe you go around the table at Thanksgiving and do this with your family, but don't ever let it be a once-a-year kind of thing. Whether in your own personal prayers or with others, tell God constantly what you're thankful for. When you're focused more on blessings than on needs and worries, you'll find yourself filled with joy!

Maybe you've heard this old hymn by Johnson Oatman or maybe not, but its words are timeless and needed still today and always!

Count your blessings, name them one by one;
Count your blessings, see what God has done;
Count your blessings, name them one by one,
And it will surprise you what the Lord has done.

Dear God, help me to focus on my blessings all the time.
You have given me so many gifts and provided for me in so
many ways, and I know You will continue. Thank You! Amen.

✣ prayer calendar ✣

We always pray and give thanks to God for you.
COLOSSIANS 1:3

Jodi loves to get on the computer and design documents using the features in Microsoft Word. Most programs like that have a calendar creator where you can choose a fun design and insert pictures and art for your own personal calendar. If you don't have access to that kind of computer program, you could simply get paper and pen and draw and design your own calendar. Once you have it designed and organized to match the year, fill it up with specific names of people to pray for! Family members, friends, neighbors, teachers, instructors, coaches, pastors and church leaders and volunteers, missionaries, health care providers—the list goes on and on! You might be surprised how quickly you get to 365 names! And if not, you can start over and list names more than once. The point is, find creative ways to remember to pray for the specific people in your life. You can never pray for anyone too much!

Dear God, help me to think of creative ways to remember people in prayer. I'm grateful for all the people You have placed in my life, and we all need You! Amen.

❧ HOW LONG? ❧

*I wait for the Lord. My soul waits
and I hope in His Word.*
PSALM 130:5

Sometimes it's really hard to be patient and wait on God's answers to prayer. In those times, we can find comfort in the fact that the prophet Habakkuk felt impatient too. He prayed, "O Lord, how long must I call for help before You will hear? I cry out to You, 'We are being hurt!' But You do not save us. Why do you make me see sins and wrong-doing? People are being destroyed in anger in front of me. There is arguing and fighting. The Law is not followed. What is right is never done. For the sinful are all around those who are right and good, so what is right looks like sin" (Habakkuk 1:2–4).

And we can learn from God's response that our human minds can never fully know and understand what God is doing in the times when it feels like He's taking much too long to answer our prayers: "Look among the nations, and see! Be surprised and full of wonder! For I am doing something in your days that you would not believe if you were told" (Habakkuk 1:5).

Dear God, help me to remember that You do things my mind can never fully understand. Help me to remember that just because I feel impatient doesn't mean You are not working out Your plans in exactly the right ways. You are good, and I trust You and hope in You. Amen.

❧ creative like your creator ❧

The LORD is the everlasting God,
the Creator of all the earth.
ISAIAH 40:28 NLT

Have you ever tried to start a project for school that needed to be really creative but you just felt totally stuck? We get it. We've been there! In those frustrating times, remember whose you are! You are a child of the almighty Creator God. Remember that after God put earth, sky, water, sun, moon, and stars in place, He created every cool plant and animal and then people. Genesis 1:27 (NLT) says, "God created human beings in his own image. In the image of God he created them; male and female he created them." Never forget that you are made in His image!

Ask Him to help you with some fresh new ideas and then keep thinking and working. You might be surprised when He answers by causing cool, creative ideas to pop into your brain!

....

Dear God, sometimes I feel like I can't think of any good ideas. Please help me when I'm stuck and frustrated. You designed me with a brain that is capable of so much. Help me to use it well and think and do like You want me to. I want to be creative like You, my amazing Creator! Amen.

❧ Love Covers ❧

*Most of all, have a true love for each
other. Love covers many sins.*
1 PETER 4:8

This scripture is one of our favorites. We're not proud of this, but Jodi and Lilly and I sometimes get angry and frustrated with each other and say and do things we later regret. Usually it's because we're not giving enough patience to each other or we're not listening well or we're letting selfishness take over. And so we find ourselves stopping to pray a lot—*God, please forgive us and help us forgive each other, and cover our mistakes with Your love and grace.* And once we pray like that, we can communicate better in peaceful ways and move forward trying to work out what's causing our conflict and unkind words and actions.

Something I remind Jodi and Lilly of all the time is that no matter what conflict we're going through, with God's help we will always work it out—because our love for each other is so great, and God's love for us is far, far greater. We never want sin to win at tearing apart our loving relationships.

*Dear Jesus, thank You most of all for Your great love.
You covered all our sin with Your blood when You took
sin upon Yourself and died on the cross. You didn't deserve
to die, but that's how much You love us! Wow! Help us to
model Your great love and grace with each other. Amen.*

☀ PUT AWAY AND PRAY ☀

*"If My people who are called by My name put away their
pride and pray, and look for My face, and turn from
their sinful ways, then I will hear from heaven.
I will forgive their sin, and will heal their land."*
2 CHRONICLES 7:14

This scripture is God's response to Solomon's prayer, but it is a response we today can learn from too. For God to answer our prayers, He wants us to put away our pride and pray, look for Him, and turn away from sin. Each time you are praying and needing God to listen and answer, you can think about this scripture and ask yourself, *Am I letting pride get in the way? Am I searching for God and His will? Do I have any sin in my life that I need to turn from and ask forgiveness for?*

Another scripture to remember is James 4:3: "Or if you do ask, you do not receive because your reasons for asking are wrong. You want these things only to please yourselves." And so you can ask yourself when you're praying, *Do I only want this to make myself happy?*

....

*Dear God, I want to make You happy with my prayers
because You are so awesome and You love me so
much. I want to look for You more than I look for
anything for myself. Please help me. Amen.*

❖ wake-up prayer ❖

*In the morning, O Lord, You will hear
my voice. In the morning I will lay my
prayers before You and will look up.*
PSALM 5:3

Isn't it neat how God made some animals like owls and bats and skunks and hedgehogs want to stay up all night and sleep all day and others that are the opposite? I'm thankful He made people different this way too. What would we do if we didn't have some people willing to work all-night jobs like in hospitals and fire stations? We should be so thankful for the differences in each person God created and how we can all work together!

Whatever time of day you love to wake up or simply have to wake up to get to school in time, start your day with prayer. Even before you get out of bed (or maybe you can roll out of bed and then kneel beside it!) ask God how you can best serve Him today, ask Him to bless you and keep you close to Him, ask Him to help you depend on His strength and power, ask Him to give you wisdom and teach you and guide you, and ask Him to help you share His love and truth with others.

....

*Dear God, each day when I wake up, no matter what
time, please help my thoughts go first to You! Show me
how to serve You each day. Please bless me and help me
to stay close to You. Please give me Your strength and
power through Your Holy Spirit. Please give me wisdom
and teach me and guide me, and help me to share
Your truth and love with those around me. Amen.*

❋ LOVE AND DISCIPLINE ❋

"Don't make light of the LORD's discipline, and don't give up when he corrects you. For the LORD disciplines those he loves, and he punishes each one he accepts as his child."
HEBREWS 12:5–6 NLT

It can be really hard to think of discipline as something to love, so we need to pray for God's help with this! Do you feel like you always accept your parents' discipline with a good attitude? For example, let's say you have a regular chore of taking care of your dog, but then you continually forget to feed and walk the pup. As a consequence, you have to miss out on a fun event. In this scenario, do you gratefully thank your parents for what you're learning in the discipline process? Hmm. . .not easy, right? But it's because good parents want their children to learn good values and work ethic that they discipline their kids. It's because they love them. And God loves you more than the very best earthly parents, and He will discipline you to correct mistakes and to guide you. So start now while you're young, praying to accept and appreciate what God is doing when He disciplines you.

Dear God, remind me that You are always loving me perfectly, even if I don't always understand or enjoy exactly what You're doing. Please help me to appreciate that You correct and guide me with good discipline! Amen.

❊ MORE ON LOVE AND DISCIPLINE ❊

*As you endure this divine discipline, remember that
God is treating you as his own children. Who ever
heard of a child who is never disciplined by its father?
If God doesn't discipline you as he does all of his children,
it means that you are illegitimate and are not really his
children at all. Since we respected our earthly fathers
who disciplined us, shouldn't we submit even more to the
discipline of the Father of our spirits, and live forever?*
HEBREWS 12:7–9 NLT

Unfortunately these days, it's pretty easy to find parents who don't discipline their children much at all. This lack of discipline often shows up in awful and chaotic ways in these families' lives. I hope you can observe this kind of thing wisely and realize why discipline is good and loving. Hebrews 12 goes on to tell us why: "God's discipline is always good for us, so that we might share in his holiness. No discipline is enjoyable while it is happening—it's painful! But afterward there will be a peaceful harvest of right living for those who are trained in this way" (Hebrews 12:10–11 NLT).

*Dear God, I want to share in Your holiness and I
want the peaceful life that comes from being trained
by discipline. So please remind me in the middle of
discipline I don't enjoy that these are the things You're
doing in my life. I am so grateful to be Your child! Amen.*

❊ ENDLESS ENERGY ❊

*Do not let yourselves get tired of doing good. If we do
not give up, we will get what is coming to us at the right
time. Because of this, we should do good to everyone.
For sure, we should do good to those who belong to Christ.*
GALATIANS 6:9–10

If we're not careful, it is really easy to get tired of doing good and making the right choices to obey God. Our
enemy wants us to believe it's too hard and too exhaust-
ing to follow Jesus. Making bad choices and acting selfishly
seems the easy, comfortable way a lot of the time. And
sometimes it is a lot easier at first, but in the long run, God's
ways are always best for us. And He will help us not to get
worn out if we ask Him. He will help us get the good kind of
rest we need (Matthew 11:28–30), and He will be the Bread
of Life (John 6:32–59) and Living Water (John 4:1–15) that
keep us going. He can give us the kind of endless energy
we need for doing the good things He has planned for us,
like doing good to others and sharing His love.

*Dear God, help me to find everything I
need in You so that I can keep doing
good and never give up. Amen.*

❧ keep Going and keep Growing ❧

*Do your best to add holy living to your faith. Then add
to this a better understanding. As you have a better
understanding, be able to say no when you need to. Do not
give up. And as you wait and do not give up, live God-like.
As you live God-like, be kind to Christian brothers and love
them. If you have all these things and keep growing in them,
they will keep you from being of no use and from having no
fruit when it comes to knowing our Lord Jesus Christ.*
2 PETER 1:5–8

Since Lilly was tiny she has always loved to meet new people
and make new friends. God has made her very social, loving
to be around people and talk to them. She has found that a
great way to use that gift is to reach out to people who look
like they might be lonely.

You might be really social too, or you might be on the
quieter side. Both are wonderful! What matters is that
you're aware of how God made you to be and ask Him to
use the personality and the gifts He's given you to serve
Him the ways He asks. And He can continually grow and
develop you with new traits and gifts and skills according
to His will, so let Him! But to do these things the best, you
need to stay in constant good relationship and communication with Him. So never stop praying. Never stop reading
God's Word. Never stop learning from and serving your loving Father!

....

*Dear God, help me to learn more about myself
and how You designed me as I keep learning
from You and staying close to You. Amen.*

❊ Take Care with Teasing ❊

Put out of your life these things also: anger, bad temper, bad feelings toward others, talk that hurts people, speaking against God, and dirty talk.
COLOSSIANS 3:8

We love fun family movies, and we love to tease. So we often find ourselves teasing each other with funny quotes from our favorite movies. The 2018 *Peter Rabbit* movie is one of our more recent favorite movies with lots of laughs.

Even though silly teasing can be so funny and fun, we do have to be careful with it. We have to think of others' feelings and not take teasing so far that it actually becomes hurtful rather than fun. Ask God to help you have wisdom with this. He loves for us to laugh and be joyful. But He wants us to encourage and build each other up with our words, not tear anyone down with thoughtless teasing.

Dear God, thank You for fun and laughter and teasing that's silly and good. But please help me to be careful never to tease so much or so carelessly that it becomes hurtful to anyone. And if I do mess up with this, please help me to sincerely apologize and ask forgiveness quickly. And if others are teasing me too much and I'm being hurt, please help me to communicate my feelings well and work it out in healthy ways. Amen.

❋ Change of Plans ❋

The mind of a man plans his way,
but the Lord shows him what to do.
PROVERBS 16:9

Has your family ever mapped out a great road trip, but then you came upon a closed highway and had to change your plans? Super frustrating! And you might never know what the problem was that closed the highway. You just know that police and safety officials who did know what was wrong closed it down. Maybe a car was on fire up ahead. Or maybe a sinkhole opened up. Yikes! (Lilly was pretty fascinated when she read a book about those recently!) Whatever the case, you made your plans and mapped out your route, but someone else changed them because they saw something you didn't and knew you would be better off not going the way you planned.

You can think of this example when you make your plans and then wonder why God doesn't help things turn out the way you thought they would or the way you worked toward. God sees and knows all, so far above and beyond what we can see. It's okay to make our plans (always asking for God's wisdom and direction as we do), but we need to work toward them while also giving them to God, praying like this:

Dear God, I need Your wisdom and direction as I make
plans. Please help them to honor You and follow Your will.
But please also help me to remember that You see so
many things about my plans that I don't, and sometimes
You change them or let changes happen to them. I might
not always understand the details, but I trust You are doing
what is best and will make everything right someday. Amen.

❧ GOD WITH YOU, HOLDING YOU ❧

"Do not fear, for I am with you. Do not be afraid, for I am your God. I will give you strength, and for sure I will help you. Yes, I will hold you up with My right hand that is right and good."
ISAIAH 41:10

We learned the absolute truth of this scripture when we went through the hardest and most confusing time we've ever known—the unexpected death of a very dear loved one. Jodi and Lilly were totally heartbroken to lose their nana, just as I was to lose my mom. But as we look back now, we see how God never left us, for sure was our Strength, and absolutely held us up and carried us when we couldn't keep going on our own. He provided love and care in so many ways and through so many people, and He still does when we feel again the grief of losing and missing her. We still don't understand why things had to happen the way they did, but we trust God anyway. We have seen His goodness and care firsthand and have felt Him so close during our worst pain. We will continue to trust Him. Isaiah 41:10 is a wonderful scripture to memorize and remember as you pray to the one true God who is your Strength and Help in any situation!

Dear God, please help me not to fear anything and to trust in Your strength no matter what. You have made me strong and carried me in the past, and I know You will continue to hold me up through any hard thing. Amen.

❄ GOD ALL-POWERFUL ❄

*Those who go to God Most High for safety
will be protected by God All-Powerful.*
PSALM 91:1 ICB

You might hear some of the news on TV or read it online or in the paper or talk about it at school, and it might scare you with stories about fighting and wars and sicknesses and crime. But never forget who your God is—the All-Powerful One! This scripture in Psalm 91 continues:

> *I will say to the Lord, "You are my place of safety
> and protection. You are my God, and I trust you."
> God will save you from hidden traps and from deadly
> diseases. He will protect you like a bird spreading its
> wings over its young. His truth will be like your armor
> and shield. You will not fear any danger by night or
> an arrow during the day. You will not be afraid of
> diseases that come in the dark or sickness that strikes
> at noon. (Psalm 91:2–6 ICB)*

There is such power in knowing and praying God's Word when you feel overcome with fear about things you cannot control. Remember that God *can* control all of it, and He loves you like crazy. Keep trusting in His love and talking to Him about everything!

*Dear God, this world is super scary sometimes. I need
You to remind me how much bigger You are than any bad
thing, and how You love and protect me. I come to You
for safety and peace, God. I love and trust You! Amen.*

❋ pray to be salt and light ❋

*"You are the salt of the earth. If salt loses its taste,
how can it be made to taste like salt again? It is no good.
It is thrown away and people walk on it. You are the light
of the world. You cannot hide a city that is on a mountain.
Men do not light a lamp and put it under a basket. They put
it on a table so it gives light to all in the house. Let your light
shine in front of men. Then they will see the good things
you do and will honor your Father Who is in heaven."*
MATTHEW 5:13–16

Maybe at your school or in your activities you feel like it's a lot easier to just stay quiet about your faith in Jesus. But that's exactly what our enemy Satan wants you to think. Jesus tells us in the Bible we should want to be like salt and light. Salt helps food taste its best, and we should want to bring out the best in others and help show them life at its best. Life at its best is a life that believes in and follows Jesus.

Jesus also wants us to be the light of the world, helping show others the way to Him. If we hide our light, we can't help others see the way to Jesus. But if we shine our lights, giving Him honor through every good thing we do, we help others honor Him too.

*Dear God, help me never to hide or be selfish with my faith
in You. I want to reach out to others and be salt and light
to them, helping them know and love You too! Amen.*

❧ The Shepherd's Leading ❧

The Lord is my Shepherd.
PSALM 23:1

If you're ever feeling stressed and anxious about anything at all, Psalm 23 offers such beautiful comfort and peace to focus on as you pray. God is your loving Shepherd, but if you're not following Him, where will you end up? But if you do let Him guide you all your life, you will find everything you need plus peace and joy no matter your circumstances.

Psalm 23 continues:

I will have everything I need. He lets me rest in fields of green grass. He leads me beside the quiet waters. He makes me strong again. He leads me in the way of living right with Himself which brings honor to His name. Yes, even if I walk through the valley of the shadow of death, I will not be afraid of anything, because You are with me. You have a walking stick with which to guide and one with which to help. These comfort me. You are making a table of food ready for me in front of those who hate me. You have poured oil on my head. I have everything I need. For sure, You will give me goodness and loving-kindness all the days of my life. Then I will live with You in Your house forever. (Psalm 23:1–6)

Dear Lord, thank You for being my Good Shepherd and providing everything I need. You calm my heart as I trust and follow You! Amen.

❋ Love Your Leaders ❋

Remember your leaders who first spoke God's Word to you.
Think of how they lived, and trust God as they did.
HEBREWS 13:7

If you're keeping a prayer journal, a great idea is to think of and list all the people who have helped and are still helping lead you in your faith. Maybe your parents or grandparents or your pastor or Sunday school teacher or VBS leader. Maybe all of the above! Thank God for these specific people and how they helped you to know God and follow Jesus. Ask Him to bless them. If you know some of their specific needs, talk to God about those. Pray for God to bring them great encouragers and ask Him how you can encourage them. Probably the best way to encourage them is to continue to live your life in obedience to God's Word as they continue to as well. God-loving leaders are rewarded richly when they are able to watch those they helped continue to follow God and do the good things He has planned. Mostly, pray for Christian leaders to continue to be strong in their faith, no matter what life brings their way, and to be leaders to others in addition to you!

Dear God, thank You for the awesome people
who have helped me to know and love You and
who keep on doing that! I am so grateful for them.
Please bless and help them in everything. Help us
to encourage each other as we live for You! Amen.

❊ POINTING TO JESUS ❊

*"You are to love each other. You must love each
other as I have loved you. If you love each other,
all men will know you are My followers."*
JOHN 13:34–35

Jodi loves learning ballet, and when she's not in class she's often dancing around our house or through a store as we're shopping. Her friend Leah told her recently, "You always stand in a ballet position," and they laughed together about it because it's often true, and Jodi hadn't really noticed! It just comes naturally now because she does ballet so often.

In a similar way, if we call ourselves followers of Jesus, others should often see us doing what Jesus says. If we've accepted Jesus as Savior and we're regularly spending time in God's Word and learning at church, then we should be doing what Jesus taught in the Bible and others should notice. We should be known for loving God first and loving others as ourselves. We should be known for being generous and helping take care of the needy. We should be known as praying people. We should be known as people who share God's truth and encourage others. We should be known as honest and fair and kind. We should never pretend to be perfect people, but we should point others to the only One who is perfect—Jesus Christ.

*Dear God, I don't want to be a fake show-off, but I
humbly want others to notice that I love You and I
follow Jesus. I know I can't follow You perfectly, but
with Your help I can do my very best. Thank You! Amen.*

☀ THE GOD WHO ANSWERS BY FIRE: PART 1 ☀

*Then the woman said to Elijah, "Now I know that
you are a man of God. Now I know that the
word of the Lord in your mouth is truth."*
1 KINGS 17:24

There is so much to learn from the prophet Elijah and the
work and miracles God did through him. His showdown with
the prophets of the false god Baal is an extraordinary true
story of the Bible. He told the people of Israel to come together at Mount Carmel and asked them,

> *"How long will you be divided between two ways of
> thinking? If the Lord is God, follow Him. But if Baal is
> God, then follow him." But the people did not answer
> him a word. Then Elijah said to the people, "I am the
> only man left who speaks for God. But here are 450
> men who speak for Baal. Bring two bulls to us. Let
> them choose one bull for themselves and cut it up
> and put it on the wood. But put no fire under it. I will
> make the other bull ready and lay it on the wood.
> And I will put no fire under it. Then you call on the
> name of your god, and I will call on the name of the
> Lord. The God Who answers by fire, He is God." All
> the people answered and said, "That is a good idea."
> (1 Kings 18:21–24)*

*Dear God, just as Elijah was known as a man of
Yours, I want to be known as a girl of Yours, and as
someone who shares truth from You. I want to help
show others that You are the one true God! Amen.*

❧ THE GOD WHO ANSWERS BY FIRE: PART 2 ❧

"The Lord, He is God. The Lord, He is God."
1 KINGS 18:39

The false god Baal had no answer for the people. So. . .

Elijah said to all the people, "Come near to me." So all the people came near to him. And he built again the altar of the Lord which had been torn down. . . . Then he set the wood in place. . . . The water flowed around the altar, and filled the ditch also. Then the time came for giving the evening gift. Elijah the man who spoke for God came near and said, "O Lord, God of Abraham, Isaac and Israel, let it be known today that You are God in Israel. Let it be known that I am Your servant, and have done all these things at Your word. Answer me, O Lord. Answer me so these people may know that You, O Lord, are God. Turn their hearts to You again." Then the fire of the Lord fell. It burned up the burnt gift, the wood, the stones and the dust. And it picked up the water that was in the ditch. All the people fell on their faces when they saw it. They said, "The Lord, He is God. The Lord, He is God." (1 Kings 18:30, 33, 35–39)

What an incredible story! I hope it gives you goose bumps!

. . . .

Dear God, like Elijah prayed, let it be known today that You are the one true God and I am Your servant. I want any good thing I do to bring praise to You and help others know You as God and Savior! Amen.

☀ The God Who Whispers Too ☀

"What are you doing here, Elijah?"
1 KINGS 19:9

After the showdown, Elijah was on the run for his life. Discouraged and alone, he had a conversation with God:

> Elijah said, "I have been very careful to serve the Lord, the God of All. For the people of Israel have turned away from Your agreement. They have torn down Your altars and have killed with the sword the men who speak for You. Only I am left, and they want to kill me." So the angel said, "Go and stand on the mountain before the Lord." And the Lord passed by. A strong wind tore through the mountains and broke the rocks in pieces before the Lord. But the Lord was not in the wind. After the wind the earth shook. But the Lord was not in the shaking of the earth. After the earth shook, a fire came. But the Lord was not in the fire. And after the fire came a sound of gentle blowing. When Elijah heard it, he put his coat over his face, and went out and stood at the opening of the hole. Then a voice came to him and said, "What are you doing here, Elijah?" (1 Kings 19:10–13)

Other versions of the Bible call the gentle blowing a whisper, and once Elijah heard from God through that whisper, he continued on with the plans God had for him!

Dear God, help me to remember that You can speak to me through anything You want, sometimes in big, dramatic ways and sometimes in quiet ways like a whisper or a gently blowing wind. No matter how You do it, I want to be listening for You and obeying You! Amen.

❊ ASKING IN HIS NAME ❊

"Whatever you ask in My name, I will do it so the shining-greatness of the Father may be seen in the Son."
JOHN 14:13

Here we are ending this book on how God can grow you as a praying girl, and the end makes us think of how prayers often end with "In Jesus' name" and then "Amen." The words of John 14:13 are the reason we often say, "In Jesus' name." Every time we pray, we should want any answer to our prayer to bring shining-greatness, or glory and praise, to God!

And *amen* is a Hebrew word meaning "truly" or "so be it" that the writers of the Bible used; we model our prayers after them when we use *amen* today. It's just a way to end our prayers with the request, *Please let what we've asked be true.*

As this book comes to a close, we want you to know we have been praying for you as you've read these devotionals. We hope you've learned a lot and had some fun reading too. We sure have!

....

Dear God, please bless each person reading this.
Let us grow closer to You through prayer. Please guide
and protect us and fill us with so much joy in knowing
You, no matter what we are going through. Help us
always to stay close to You as we learn from You and
live for You because of Jesus our Savior. Amen.

scripture index

OLD TESTAMENT